TO THE POINT

Dale C. Spartas (signature)

DALE C. SPARTAS

TOM DAVIS

Foreword by
Guy de la Valdène

Dave,

Thanks for supporting PLWA.

Wishing you great dog work & stylish points.

yours in Conservation

Dale (signature)

wishing you great dog work with Scooter.

STACKPOLE BOOKS

TO THE POINT
A Tribute to Pointing Dogs

Published by
STACKPOLE BOOKS
5067 Ritter Road
Mechanicsburg, PA 17055
www.stackpolebooks.com

Custom prints and photography are available from
Dale C. Spartas
DCS Photo, Inc.
PO Box 1367
Bozeman, MT 59771
phone (406) 585-2244
fax (406) 585-0038
www.spartasphoto.com
email *spartasphoto@imt.net*

Printed in China

First edition

10 9 8 7 6 5 4 3 2 1

Library of Congress Cataloging-in-Publication Data
Spartas, Dale C.
    To the point : a tribute to pointing dogs / Dale Spartas, Tom Davis ;
  with a foreword by Guy de la Valdene.— 1st ed.
      p.   cm.
    ISBN 0-8117-0043-7 (hardcover)
    1. Pointing dogs.   2. Pointing dogs—Pictorial works.   3. Photography
of dogs.   I. Davis, Tom, 1956–   II. Title.
SF428.5 .S64   2003
636.752'5—dc21
                                                                    2003003857

To Zack and Emmylou, my partners, teachers, and muses. The birds they pointed were the least of what they gave me. And to Robert G. Wehle, the greatest pointing dog man of all, who exemplified class in every word and deed, and whose unwavering devotion to the highest ideals of sportsmanship is a legacy that will forever burn bright.

—*Tom Davis*

It seems like yesterday, but it was a warm July morning in 1961. My sister Darlene and I were sitting on the front porch eating cereal when Uncle Joe's Oldsmobile rumbled up the driveway in a cloud of dust. Mom was not home, which I suspect was part of the plan.

Uncle Joe, smoking a big cigar, quickly got out of the car.

"Dale and Darlene, come over here—I've something I want to show you," he said. He went to the back of the Eighty-Eight, opened the trunk, and took out a big cardboard box.

"Go ahead and open it," he said. Sitting in the corner of the box looking up at us was the cutest and most beautiful tricolor puppy we'd ever seen, a childhood dream come true.

"Who does the puppy belong to?" we asked.

"To you if you want it," Uncle Joe replied.

Did we want it? Are you kidding? Uncle Joe reached into the box with one of his massive hands, picked up the puppy, and handed her to Darlene.

"Ladies before gentlemen," Uncle Joe cautioned.

Once in Darlene's arms, the scared pup turned into a tail-wagging, face-licking ball of happiness. Mom didn't have a chance. We had the puppy for three hours before she came home, and once Mom saw the pup she couldn't resist either.

Did God create puppies for children? Or were children created for puppies? Either way there is no better fit. Spotty became my fishing, trapping, and hunting partner, my protector and best friend. We were inseparable. The ultimate versatile dog, she'd catch muskrats, tree squirrels, and coons, run rabbits, and flush birds. When she started a rabbit she'd bay like a hound. When trailing pheasants, grouse, or woodcock, she would get birdy and work like a Labrador or spaniel. Her reputation preceded her, and members of the Stamford Fish & Game Club would pick her up and take her hunting while I was in school. She was a great dog and the best friend a boy could have.

This book is dedicated to a little black, brown, and white dog named Spot.

—*Dale C. Spartas*

Contents

Photographer's Preface

Dogs have always been a big part of my life. My family and friends upon seeing me with a pup or dog always said I had a way with them. But this book is not about me. *To the Point* is a tribute to the desire, determination, spirit, stamina, instinct, and beauty of pointing dogs. Any pointing dog man will tell you that the best part of a hunt is the dogs. They say there are no absolutes in life, but among dog people there are several common denominators that hold true and fast. The first is they love dogs and dog work. The second is they would rather not hunt than hunt without a dog.

Over the years I have been owned by eleven dogs of six different breeds. Each dog is distinctly different from the others, each exhibits individual personality and breed characteristics.

All dogs, if given the chance, love to hunt because the hunting instinct is innate in all dogs. Selective breeding has bestowed today's sporting dogs with superior genetics, resulting in heightened instinct, intensity, and seemingly incomprehensible stamina.

The photography in this book is a compilation of twenty-four years behind the camera and thousands upon thousands of frames of which one

out of every hundred photographs may have made it into the final edit. The imagery selected for *To the Point* attempts to capture the exuberance, talent, and magnificence of pointing dogs. I hope these images will take you afield and allow you to experience the speed, stamina, and thrill of a brace of bird dogs flashing through the pines or across the horizon on a frosty morning. My hope is that these photographs portray the beauty, intensity, and essence of a hard point. Finally, I hope to show the many aspects of training, trialing, hunting, and living with pointing dogs. Let us lift our glasses and toast these incredible animals . . . *To the Point.*

—Dale C. Spartas

Foreword

The thrill of owning a pointing dog that takes care of business correctly is intimate and all-embracing. We who love these dogs live to witness their age-old predatory instincts of momentarily pausing before leaping, their every fiber alert with high energy. Whether in the sagebrush hills of the West, the tag-alders of the Midwest, or the broom-sedge fields of the South, a dog on point imposes his will on the natural world and fills the surrounding space with intensity and his master with a sense of pride and incredulity.

The agony of owning a pointing dog that does not take care of business is a torment that owners around the world deal with on a daily basis. Whereas a dog on point stands at the right hand of Zeus, a dog on the loose runs with Lucifer.

Photography is the medium with which Dale C. Spartas has captured the kingdom of dogs. His love for the environment and his love for the camera are one. Every image in *To the Point* is a piece of the mosaic that makes up that particular breed. Spartas's work depicts the relationship of dogs to the world in which they live and the masters they serve. Like all good photographers, Spartas achieves intimacy with his subjects, a depth of purpose, and a momentary truth that are apparent in every picture. His dogs look out on us calmly, exultant in the thrill of discovery and secure in

Acknowledgments

I would like to acknowledge and thank the following people: Gasper & Ruth Accardi, Galt Allee, David Baker, Gary & Marcy Bateman, Hans Boye Boyesen, Dennis & Veronica Bene, Frank & Kathy Calta, Dick Chapman, Peter & Diane Clarke, George, Mark & Pete Connell, Tim Crawford, Howard Davis, Tom Davis, Brian Dunn, Joe Edwards, Brad Ehrnmin, Ed Epsen, Tom Eversman, Brian Fay, Mike & Loretta Gaddis, Allan Gadourey, Paul Giesenhagen & Family, Dave & Sissy Girtman, Ed Gray, Peter Gurney, Charlie Harvey, Gordon & Alice Hurd, Alfred & Craig Janssen, Paul T. Jones, Roger Keckiessen, David & Julie Kirkland, Conrad & Tana Kradolfer, Tim Leary, Ted Lundrigan, Kerry Malloy, T. R. & Dan McClellan, Michael McGuire, Michael McIntosh, Tracy & Wynell Marquis, Dave Maynard, John Millington, Missouri Headwaters Gun Dog Club, Shawn McNeely, Allen Neelley, Butch Nelson, Donal & Katie O'Brien, Donal O'Brien III, Steve Owen, Datus Proper, David Richards, Jerry Robinson, Dave Sharpe, Roger Sparks, Matt Sullivan, Sallie Sullivan, Dale Sweetser, John & Ike Todd, Van Der Beek Family, Peter Weber, Jeff Whiddon, Ted Wilbert, Rusty Wilson, Denis Witmer, Scott Wuebber, Don Zahourek, and all their beautiful dogs.

If I neglected to mention anyone, please forgive me. The years, miles, faces, places, and dogs have been many.

—*Dale C. Spartas*

the knowledge that we love them. These dogs are not isolated from their universe but profoundly related to it.

A photographer is a researcher using resources and techniques to delve into the truth and meaning of the world he lives in. Dale C. Spartas has been exploring the world of dogs for a quarter of a century. For this book he has presented a collection of pictures that praise his craft and his insight. The accompanying text by his collaborator, Tom Davis, is a fitting complement to the various breeds under consideration.

With these new portraits of pointing dogs, Dale has thoughtfully recorded the tacit bond between man and his favorite hunting companion. These are pictures of dogs waiting to be released, graceful dogs in motion, dogs pausing to survey their territory, dogs watchfully facing the unknown, and dogs daydreaming in moments that are outside time. If you care about dogs, these photographs will strike an emotional chord.

Thoreau said, "You cannot say more than you can see." As you turn the pages of *To the Point*, you'll discover an honest and forceful vision that is art.

—*Guy de la Valdène*

THE POINTER IS THE BIRD DOG LAID BARE, A single-minded, laser-focused specialist, a high-performance engine in a lean, hard, stripped-down body. Everything about it is close to the bone. Its speed is blinding; its stamina, fueled by an all but unfathomable reservoir of desire, is astonishing. To watch a pointer in action, rimming the field edges with its graceful, ground-devouring stride, muscles rippling, tail describing flourishes in the air like a conductor's baton, is to be mesmerized. And to see it strike point, colliding with the fugitive scent of *bird!* as if it were a stone wall and being transformed, in the blink of an eye, from pure dynamism to living statuary, is to witness one of the most breathtaking acts in the universe of sport—and one of the most definitive.

The white-hot intensity of the pointer's resolve serves as a reminder that the centuries of selective breeding are, in a sense, a veneer, and that the instinct to hunt and find birds is, ultimately, rooted in the instinct to survive. We like to say that the pointer lives to hunt, but in fact it's the other way around. At the ancient, immutable core of the pointer's predator soul, it hunts to live.

The Pointer

THE POINTER is an acknowledged marvel of athleticism, a remarkable combination of diverse natural abilities and finely honed skills. Indeed, there are those who claim that no athlete on earth, two-legged or four-, can match the pointer's sheer physical prowess. When you consider the things pointers do and the places and conditions in which they do them—a crude analogy would be running cross-country at top speed while keeping your eyes peeled for edible mushrooms—it's hard to refute the argument.

EVERYTHING THE POINTER DOES, it does at one speed: flat out. This includes retrieving, although it must be conceded that it's not the breed's strong suit. Every now and then you run across a pointer that's born as eager to retrieve as a Labrador, but the breed in general tends to be indifferent toward the act; obsessed with finding live birds, marginally interested (at best) in scooping up those that fall to the gun. This is why, when you see a pointer that retrieves as if it's been shot out of a cannon, the chances are very good that it's a graduate of "force breaking," a process that sounds harsher than it is—assuming, of course, that the student doesn't have a skull as thick as an anvil.

FOR THE SAME REASONS that the pointer is the breed of choice for bird hunting in big country, it's the dominant force in horseback field trials, uniquely American competitions that began in the late-nineteenth century as an offshoot of the horseback quail hunting practiced in the South. These events place a premium on torrid pace and extreme range; in fact, a famous definition of a great field trial dog is "a dog that runs off—but not quite." Sometimes, though, they *do* run off—or, in field trial terminology, get out of pocket—forcing their handlers to go looking for them. Fortunately, the availability of radio-tracking technology, a.k.a. telemetry, has made locating lost dogs a lot faster and easier than it used to be. That's what this handler, Robin Gates, is doing: using a portable antenna to home in on a radio signal (audible as a beep) emitted by a special collar.

THE POINTER MAY BE THE BIRD DOG NONPAREIL, but this doesn't mean, alas, that it ignores every other critter that it runs across or, more accurately, that its nose detects. Scent is the pointer's primary means of apprehending and understanding the world around it (as it is for all dogs). By the same token, there's also a deep, fundamental level at which the "prey drive" is indiscriminate. When this drive is as powerful as it is in the pointer, bad things can happen—a tussle with a porcupine being one of them. The good news is that one such encounter is usually enough to effect a permanent cure (although some dogs are chronic recidivists), and if the quills are removed promptly the dog will likely suffer nothing more serious than a temporary loss of dignity.

A POINTER IN THE FIELD is never truly relaxed. It's a compressed spring tensed to uncoil, a smoldering ember awaiting only the tinder of a word to burst into flame. When it does, even the biggest country—like this stubble field in the shadow of the mountains, a place that fairly screams *Hungarian partridge!*—seems barely of a size to contain the blaze. At its thrilling best, a pointer has the ability to fill the landscape with its presence.

THIS POINTER'S UPTILTED HEAD indicates that she's catching scent—"winding" the birds, as it's often called—a good distance away. Experienced hunters learn to read their dogs' attitudes on point, gleaning from their posture and intensity how far or near the birds are likely to be and whether they're running or holding. This information, in turn, helps the hunter anticipate the flush and position himself advantageously for the shot. It's far from an exact science, however.

POINTERS ARE PRIMARILY associated with big country, places like the high plains of the West and the savannahs of south Texas where their great speed, range, and stamina give them a decided edge over other breeds. Given the opportunity and training, however, they also excel as cover dogs, tearing through the briars, brambles, and thickets in search of woodcock and ruffed grouse—and belying the skimpy protection afforded by their short coats. For a pointer with birds on his mind, losing a little hair—if not a little blood—is all in a day's work.

PINEY WOODS, russet sedge fields, and a brace of stylish pointers: When you say bobwhite quail hunting, this is the image that unfailingly leaps to the mind's eye. Indeed, the pointer and the bobwhite quail are as closely conjoined in the imagination as Astaire and Rogers, their pairing among the most resonant in all of sport. Here, the dog closer to the hunter has the find; the other dog is honoring, or backing, its bracemate's point—although it appears to have taken its own sweet time doing so.

POINTING DOGS AND STANDING CORN are a recipe for disaster. Corn that's been recently combined, though, is a different story—especially if the stalks aren't cut. With plenty of waste corn scattered around the field and enough overhead cover to offer a measure of security, such a field will attract pheasants the way celebrities attract paparazzi. And while pheasants are in some ways the most difficult quarry of all for a pointing dog—they have this annoying habit of refusing to stay put—if any breed is up to the task, it's the pointer. Old-time authorities often spoke of dogs that could "overawe" pheasants (and other birds) into holding, hitting them so hard and fast that they were pinned down as if by an invisible force—and no breed hits its birds harder and faster than the pointer.

SOME POINTER OWNERS don't make an issue of retrieving; as long as their dogs point dead or otherwise lead them to the downed birds, they're perfectly happy. For others, though, a dog that retrieves promptly, reliably, and tenderly to hand is an integral part of the experience. You might say that it completes the circle.

STEEPED IN TRADITION and burnished by the patina of romance, plantation-style bob-white quail hunting is as much a part of southern culture as cotillions and courtly manners (although its roots trace back to carpetbagging Yankees who amassed large land holdings after the Civil War). Make no mistake, however: The Tennessee walking horses and shooting wagons aren't mere ornaments. The walking horses help the dog handlers keep tabs on wide-ranging pointers; the wagons, in addition to providing a comfortable ride for the gunners, serve as portable kennels.

THE CLASSIC PLANTATION-STYLE QUAIL HUNT follows established routes known as courses. Each course takes about three hours to complete; the usual procedure is to hunt the morning course, return to the lodge for lunch (and maybe a siesta), then head out again on the afternoon course. Most handlers use two or even three braces of pointers per course, hunting one brace at a time and rotating them at intervals to keep them fresh—hence the reason for the dog boxes built into the shooting wagon.

SOUTH OF THE MASON-DIXON
line, the terms "bird dog" and
"pointer" are synonymous.
(Yankee ears are likely to hear
them pronounced *buhd dawg*
and *p'inter.*) Other breeds
are referred to by their proper
names—on the rare occasions
they enter the discussion at all.

HORSES AND POINTERS are another of those evocative
combinations. And, in fact, the horse played a key
role in the pointer's transformation from a rather slow,
cumbersome, methodical worker (as it was described
in the mid-nineteenth century by Frank Forester,
America's first important outdoor writer) to the
ground-devouring, horizon-scorching whirlwind of
today. The horse, by enabling the sportsman to cover
more ground and see much farther than he could on
foot, originally brought the fleeter, wider-ranging kind
of pointing dog into vogue; then, as horseback field
trials began to drive pointer breeding (the sires heavily
patronized by breeders are almost invariably field trial
champions), the modern pointer "type" became established. That aside, roading dogs from horseback, as
this trainer is doing, also happens to be a terrific way
to get them in shape—and keep them there.

It's rare to see any breed other than a pointer in a plantation shooting dog string, but when you do it's invariably an English setter. And, as this gunner has discovered, quail are challenging enough to hit without having to contend with trees in your way. A pointer is capable of wondrous feats, but you still have to shoot the birds yourself.

WHEN A DOG has willfully and knowingly misbehaved—broken point and flushed the birds, for example—it's important not only to get your hands on the offender as quickly as possible, but to return him to the scene of the crime to administer the proper correction. This is another area in which a horse can be a great training aid, giving you a leg up, so to speak, in what could otherwise turn out to be a protracted chase. Even in plantation country, though, you sometimes have no recourse but to ride "shank's mare"—go it afoot, that is—and hope for the best.

THERE IS NO STAGE to compare with a well-managed quail plantation for showcasing a pointer's skills. And the single most useful tool plantation managers have at their disposal for optimizing bobwhite quail habitat—and, in turn, bird numbers—is controlled burning. These burns, carried out in the late winter and early spring, serve to clear the ground of accumulated thatch (quail like to feel the earth under their feet), suppress woody vegetation, and stimulate the growth of desirable grasses and forbs.

THESE POINTERS ARE CLEARLY an experienced pair, wise in the ways of the bobwhite quail. Not only has the dog in the foreground stylishly and intently honored its bracemate's point, it's done so at a respectful distance. And well that it has, because a covey of bobs "caught out" in this skimpy cover—the birds had likely left the sanctuary of the hardwood bottom to feed along the field edge—is apt to flush at the slightest provocation. In other words, one step more would be one step too many.

"PATTERN" IS ONE of the most important words in the pointing dog lexicon. Simply stated, it refers to the way the dog works the country. A dog that runs a good pattern stays to the front, keeps tabs on its handler's whereabouts, uses the wind to its advantage whenever possible, adjusts its range to the nature of the terrain and the density of the cover (closer in heavy cover, wider in thin cover), and industriously searches the birdy places. When these places—"objectives," dog people call them—are scattered across the landscape, the dog should choose them intelligently and go to them boldly. And, just as importantly, the dog's handler should give him the freedom to do so, trusting in the dog's blood, training, and experience.

THIS IS THE PAYOFF, the electric moment when training, experience, and opportunity come together, when the dogs have done their part and now it's up to *you*. It is, after all, a partnership and has been since long before sportsmen began "shooting flying" circa 1600 or so. Wingshooting over pointers is perhaps the most highly developed, most artful form of hunting there is, but the taproot still reaches back thousands of years to the time when a few canny wolves figured out that humans could be useful to them—and vice-versa.

HANDLING A DOG in the field is more than tooting a whistle and uttering an occasional command. It's also a matter of management: knowing your dog's abilities and limitations, keeping it out of harm's way, doing your part to help it perform at its best. For example, if you're hunting in warm weather or in an area where your dog can't get an occasional drink, it's a smart idea to carry water—and a really dumb one not to. Dogs have only a limited capacity to dissipate body heat, and when they're exerting themselves in hot, dry conditions, they need to be watered frequently. Every year pointing dogs whose owners aren't properly vigilant die or suffer permanent injury from heat-related illness.

POINTERS HAVE THE REPUTATION for being cool, aloof, and undemonstrative. Some are, certainly: They regard their owners/handlers/trainers not so much as friends but as facilitators, or maybe business partners—the business in this case being bird hunting. But while pointers are temperamentally better suited to this kind of impersonal, professional relationship than other pointing breeds—one of the biggest reasons they're preferred by field trial trainers who, out of necessity, maintain large strings of dogs—by and large they're as appreciative as any dog of a warm word and an affectionate caress.

FOOLING WITH PUPPIES is not just a pleasant diversion. The more human contact they have—and the more environments and experiences they're exposed to—the better equipped they are, psychologically, to accept training and, in particular, to mature into the kinds of dogs that hunt boldly and independently while remaining responsive to their handlers.

THESE SEVEN-WEEK-OLD PUPS are ready to go to their new homes. Research has shown that the puppy's brain and nervous system become fully mature at about forty-nine days old, and that this is the optimum time for a pup to leave its littermates and begin to develop a bond with its human family. This does *not* mean, however, that you should be leery about acquiring an older puppy. As long as the pup comes from good stock and has been given lots of TLC by the breeder—"socialization," in dog-speak—you've got nothing to worry about.

REAMS OF COPY have been devoted to the subject of how to pick a puppy. But it's really pretty simple: You pick the puppy's *parents*. Once you've found the right sire–dam combination—the right litter, in other words—the only criteria of any importance are whether you want a male or a female and what your color preference is. Beyond that, you might as well play a hunch.

NO BREED is as outstandingly precocious as the pointer. Many pointer pups will sight point as soon as they're able to walk, styling up impressively on bumble-bees, butterflies, scudding leaves, or just about anything else that captures their attention.

ALTHOUGH EVERY PUP matures at a slightly different rate—and while all display a measure of comic ungainliness—an occasional pup is uncommonly well coordinated for its age. Dog people refer to this as being "collected," meaning that there is very little superfluous movement, and that all the limbs seem to be working toward the same purpose. Collected or not, plenty of exercise is essential to the development of every pup.

OPINION IS SHARPLY DIVIDED regarding the familiar ritual of flicking a wing in front of a puppy to trigger a point. Some contend that it's merely a parlor trick, that it serves no useful purpose and may in fact inhibit the pup's development by encouraging it to point by sight rather than by scent. The pro-wing camp argues that it's a valuable tool for the assessment of precocity and that, judiciously employed, it can serve as a foundation for later training refinements, such as teaching a dog to hunt close. The late Robert G. Wehle, whose Elhew Kennels set the standard in pointer breeding for over half a century, always put great stock in the wing's utility.

POINTER PUPPIES tend to be indiscriminate about the things they point. The list is literally endless—although soap bubbles have to be counted among the more unusual items.

IF YOU THROW SOMETHING that a puppy can get into its mouth, whether a bumper, a tennis ball, or an old glove, he'll invariably pick it up and carry it around. If the pup brings it back, praise him to high heaven—and count your blessings, because you just might have a natural retriever on your hands. Of course, if there's any competition in the vicinity, you're in for a lengthy game of keep-away.

WALKING PUPS in the field serves a number of purposes beyond giving them their daily exercise. By working the pups in the right kinds of cover and gently guiding them to the places where game is likely to be found, a savvy trainer can make great strides in the development of their pattern, handling response, and bird sense—the knack some dogs seem to have not just for knowing where to find birds, but how to get them pointed. In this as in so many other areas of pointing dog training, experience is the best teacher.

IF THERE'S A SINGLE BEDROCK COMPONENT of pointing dog performance, it's staunchness—
staying resolutely on point (not breaking point) while the gunner attempts to flush the birds.
All else equal, staunchness is what spells the difference between a dog you can pleasantly and
productively hunt over and one that remains a work in progress. Here, the trainer steadies a
young pointer—encourages his staunchness—by restraining him lightly with one hand, styling
him up with the other, and softly repeating the "whoa" command. It's critical at this stage *not*
to shoot any birds until and unless the dog stays staunch; to do otherwise would essentially be
to reinforce an undesirable behavior.

A NATIVE OF THE EURASIAN STEPPES, the gray partridge, commonly called the Hungarian partridge, was introduced to North America in the early 1900s. While there are scattered pockets of Huns as far east as Prince Edward Island, the bird's stronghold is the semi-arid grasslands of the American West and the Canadian prairie provinces, the kind of wide-open country that demands a big-going dog—a bill that the pointer is more likely to fill than any other breed.

THE FIRST STEP in force-breaking a dog to retrieve is simply teaching it to take an object—either a wooden buck or, as here, a canvas-covered dummy—hold it in its mouth, and keep it there until ordered to release it. The next step is getting the dog, upon command, to pick the dummy off the ground. Building on this, you gradually lengthen the distance the dog has to travel to pick up the dummy, until it will reliably do so wherever it falls. All that remains then is convincing the dog to bring the dummy back.

A BRASS BELL is the traditional tool for keeping track of a dog in tight grouse and woodcock cover, cover in which the dog is out of sight more often than not—and should be, if it's doing its job. The contemporary, high-tech method is the electronic beeper. Available since the early 1980s, it has the advantage of remaining audible when the dog points, thus eliminating the guesswork (and reducing the time) involved in finding it. The beeper's shrill tone is not as pleasant to the human ear as the tinkling of a bell, however, which is why some hunters take a best-of-both-worlds approach, using a bell in tandem with a beeper set on the point-signal-only mode.

IN THE POPULAR IMAGINATION, the lifted forepaw is the signature of a dog on point—not the rigid tail, not the transfixed gaze, not the quivering nostrils. Artists often lift a forepaw in their depictions of pointing dogs; cartoonists *always* do. The thing is, art does not necessarily imitate life, and while it may be the classic stance, it occurs somewhat less frequently than you might suspect. Certain dogs, irrespective of breed, seem to be predisposed to it; many will lift a forepaw on occasion; some insist on keeping all four feet firmly planted. A dog that catches scent mid-stride may even point with a lifted hind paw.

"GROUND COVERAGE" is a term that means pretty much what you'd think it does. It's closely related to pattern, but whereas pattern is a qualitative measure, ground coverage is quantitative. In other words, the question isn't "How?" but "How much?" And pointers, by dint of their unsurpassed speed, stamina, and desire, in general cover more ground than any other pointing breed. This is also the reason that the pointer can be too much dog for the sportsman who prefers a slower, closer-working, more tractable canine gunning partner.

THE POINT, when you stop to analyze it, serves several purposes. For starters, it indicates the presence of game—that's a given. It also indicates the location of said game, although the vagaries of scent and of the birds' behavior can make this an exercise in informed speculation. Every hunter has had the experience of kicking the cover where the dog says they are to no avail, only to flush the birds behind, off to the side, or even directly underneath the point. When you see the blazing intensity and resolve displayed by this pointer, however, you're tempted to bet the pot that the birds are *right there*—and you're reminded of the observation that the point, above all else, is a bridge between worlds: the bird dog's world of scent and our human world of sight. It's a miraculous feat, this straddling of dimensions; some might even call it magic.

THE SETTERS—ENGLISH, IRISH, GORDON—
are the acknowledged aristocracy of bird dogs.
Regal on point and incomparably graceful
in action, they strike the perfect balance of form and
function. True, other breeds may match or even at
times surpass them when the performance is judged
solely on technical merit—every dog has its day, as
they say—but when style is the criterion, setters rule.
A fiery setter slashing the cover, eyes burning with
purpose, proud flag hoisted skyward, is class person-
ified. Little wonder that it's said a good setter will
spoil you for any other breed, or that what America's
first important outdoor writer, Frank Forester,
declared some 150 years ago remains a widely held
opinion: "First in the list of sporting dogs, without
a moment's hesitation, I place the setter."

And yet, somewhat paradoxically, the setters are
the most individualistic, most resistant to generaliza-
tion, of all the pointing dogs. Do they find more birds
than other breeds? Sometimes—but not always. Do
they have more appealing personalities? Often—but
not necessarily. Are they easier to train and to handle?
Well, that depends. Ultimately, asking why men and
women are drawn to setters is like asking them why
they're drawn to green eyes or crooked smiles. They
just are.

This much is certain: Once a setter truly captures
your imagination, you are never again free.

The Setters

OF THE THREE SETTER BREEDS, the English setter is far and away the most popular among American sportsmen. In fact, when gun dog people use the word "setter" without prefix, ninety-nine times out of one hundred they're referring to the English variety. A biddable, versatile bird-finder blessed with a rugged constitution, eye-catching way of going, and an affectionate personality, it's proven its mettle, time and time again, in every upland hunting situation the continent has to offer. The English setter has prospered, too, thanks to generations of breeders who kept their eyes on the ball and rigorously selected their breeding stock for ability in the field, not merely for appearance.

IN THE EIGHTEENTH AND EARLY NINETEENTH CENTURIES, a number of landed British sportsmen developed distinctive lines of setters, mingling and refining the blood of various individual dogs until a definite type was established. Collectively, these lines were known as the Castle strains—and the most famous of all was the one developed by a Scottish nobleman, the fourth Duke of Gordon, in the late-1700s. Imported to America in the mid-1800s, the Gordon setter was embraced in particular by market hunters, for whom the breed's close-working style, unusual stamina, and devotion to its master were ideally suited. Like the Irish setter, however, the Gordon fell out of favor, became a victim of its own beauty, and for most of the twentieth century was bred almost exclusively for the show ring. The good news is that the Gordon has made a comeback, and that there are now a number of breeders producing fine black and tans, as they're often called, for the field.

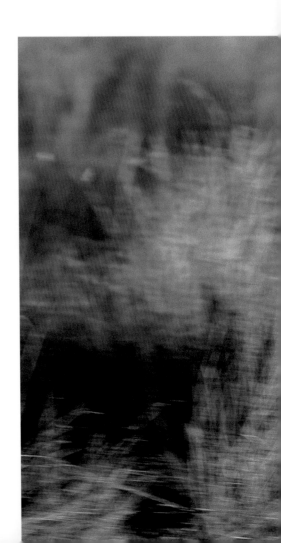

HISTORICALLY, THE IRISH SETTER didn't give an inch to its English cousin: In a legendary two-day match race held in Alabama in 1879, the Irish setter Joe Jr. defeated Gladstone, the most famous English setter of the time, sixty-one quail finds to fifty-two. By the turn of the century, however, the red dogs were no longer in vogue with hunters, and as their breeding was increasingly co-opted by the show fancy (whose ideal was, and is, an arbitrary standard of beauty), the qualities that served them well in the uplands all but vanished. Recognizing that the hunting Irish setter was on the verge of extinction, in the early 1950s a group of sportsmen, organized under the banner of the National Red Setter Field Trial Club, dedicated itself to what it termed "The Purest Challenge": the breed's restoration as a useful gun dog. The long and short of it is that the sportsmen succeeded.

NO BREED IS MORE STRONGLY identified with ruffed grouse than the English setter. It's long been the traditional choice for hunting this King of Game Birds—so long, in fact, that many sportsmen take the English setter–ruffed grouse equation as received wisdom, accepting it without question or qualification. But there are good, valid reasons why the breed makes superior grouse dogs. For one, the English setter tends to have a natural quartering (sweeping from side to side) pattern, generally accepted as the most efficient way to canvass the brushy woodlands favored by grouse. For another, it attacks the cover fearlessly, protected from briars and thorns by its long coat. Finally, the English setter possesses a wealth of that elusive commodity known as bird sense, an instinctive understanding of when to approach its game boldly, and when to proceed with caution.

WHILE RUFFED GROUSE AND WOODCOCK are often found in the same cover, their behavior could hardly be more different. Quick to flush at the merest hint of danger, the grouse is among the most difficult birds for a dog to point, its credo being that it is better to live very nervously than not at all. The woodcock, in contrast, prefers to sit tight, hoping that danger passes it by, and as a result is generally considered the easiest bird of all for a pointing dog to handle. Experienced grouse and woodcock hunters are sometimes able to tell by their dog's attitude which of the birds it's pointing, and position themselves accordingly: Grouse tend to flush farther out and stay relatively low; woodcock tend to flush close and go out high. Over the long haul, though, the safest course is to be ready for whatever pops up.

RAPPORT IS AN OFT-USED WORD in the pointing dog lexicon. All bird dogs profit from a close rapport with their handler—it's what gives them the confidence to hunt boldly and independently while remaining bidda-ble—but for setters, with their sensitive personalities, it's essential. This is especially true in thick grouse and woodcock cover, where dog and handler are rarely in sight of one another, and a premium is placed on making as little noise as possible. A grouse-savvy setter seems able to read its handler's mind.

THIS RUGGEDLY HANDSOME devil has the classic English setter look: deep, square muzzle; dark nose and eyes; broad skull with a well-defined stop; silky, well-set ears. The overall expression is one of soulful intelligence—and unquestioned capability. The bell on his neck tells you that he's well acquainted with ruffed grouse, woodcock, and the demands of their pursuit.

OF COURSE, THE SAME COAT that repels briars and provides an insulating layer against the cold attracts burrs like nobody's business. Setter owners consider the necessity of post-hunt grooming a small price to pay; most of them, in fact, rather enjoy it. Their dogs certainly do.

THE NUMBER OF BIRDS in the bag should never be the most important criterion for measuring a hunt's success. Pointing dog people, who place equal if not greater emphasis on their dog's performance than they do on their own, are particularly inclined to this view— and setter people most of all. To the men and women in thrall to setters, upland bird hunting in partnership with their adored dogs is something very much like an art, a perpetual striving toward perfection. This does not mean, however, that every once in a blue moon you don't end up with one heck of a bunch of birds—or that these days don't stand out a little more prominently in the landscape of memory.

STRICTLY IN THE CONTEXT of upland bird hunting, the English setter is arguably the most versatile of all the pointing breeds. It has the intelligence, the athletic ability, and the bred-in-the-bone instincts to adjust its range and pattern in response to the nature of the terrain, and—given proper exposure and experience—to successfully handle a variety of game birds. Every dog has a different learning curve in this respect—but it helps to have the right stuff to begin with.

OVER THE COURSE of a day's hunt, it's a good idea
to stop every so often, call in the dog(s), and take a
short break. Relaxing for a few minutes gives everyone
a chance to rest their legs, catch their breath, grab a
drink and maybe a snack, and return to the field mentally and physically refreshed. Setters always seem to
appreciate a little sugar, too.

IN HIS FAMOUS *Meditations on Hunting*, the Spanish philosopher Ortega y Gasset observed that it is the natural condition of game to be scarce. Applied to pointing dogs, this means that they're destined to spend a lot more time running than they are actually standing on point. It also means that hunters are destined to spend the majority of their time *watching* the dogs run. Setter breeders figured this out a long time ago and endowed their dogs with the speed, fluidity, and eye-catching animation that make them a pleasure to behold on the ground. The exuberance—and the desire—were *always* there.

THIS SETTER'S TENSED, low-in-front posture indicates that it hit scent hard and suddenly, literally reflexing onto point, and that the birds—Hungarian partridge or possibly sharp-tailed grouse—are very close. The gunner had better be on his toes, because the flush is going to come sooner rather than later.

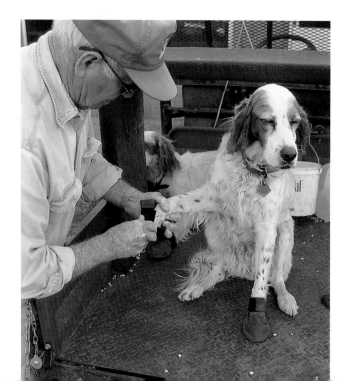

YOU DON'T SEE a lot of setters in the strings of Texas and Desert Southwest quail hunters—it's pointer country, mostly—but the ones you *do* see tend to be several notches above ordinary, possessing the range, stamina, and ability to handle the warm weather that the terrain and climate demand. Handling cactus, sandspurs, and the myriad other sharp, spiny, prickly stuff that abound in that part of the world is quite another matter, however. Dog boots do a fine job protecting pads from punctures and abrasions, but they're ultimately a necessary evil—as if you couldn't tell by the expression of stoic resignation worn by this lady setter.

HORSEBACK FIELD TRIALS are another realm in which setters are comparatively rare. Pointers dominate the sport; among other reasons, they're generally faster to mature and reach their peak, and in the field trial game, time, as they say, is money. Still, there are always enough competitive English setters being campaigned to keep things interesting, and by most accounts they win as many placements, on a per capita basis, as pointers do. His coat trimmed close save for a fringe of feathering on his tail, this leggy charger stands ready to be turned loose at the breakaway of the prestigious Masters Open Shooting Dog Championship near Albany, Georgia.

WHEN YOU SEE A SETTER riding in the seat next to its owner, you can bet that they're a team to be reckoned with. At the risk of sounding like a broken record, while it's desirable to spend as much time as possible with your dog regardless of breed, it's critically important with setters. A setter will simply not reach its maximum potential as a bird dog unless—or until—a bond of trust is forged between it and its owner.

STRIVING TO ESTABLISH A BOND or develop a rapport is all well and good—but don't be surprised if your dog assumes an aura of entitlement and begins to push the envelope. In this as in every relationship, there are certain lines that shouldn't be crossed.

With their fuzzy ears, pudgy legs, squished-up faces, and quizzical expressions, English setter puppies are so damnably irresistible that there ought to be a law. It certainly doesn't make picking the one you want to take home any easier—although if you've done the home-work necessary to ensure that you're making your choice from the right kennel, bloodline, and litter, you really can't go wrong.

MOST ENGLISH SETTER PUPPIES will point a wing at a young age. But while their willingness to do so is a reliable indicator of precocity, some slow-to-mature pups—usually males—display little or no interest in this game. Not to worry: If your pup comes from solid hunting stock, the light will go on once it gets a few nosefuls of the real thing. In this as in so many other aspects of dog training, patience is its own reward.

WHILE IT'S POSSIBLE that this uncommonly well-conformed pup is sight-pointing a songbird perched on a limb, it's more likely that she's looking to her alpha human for a sight cue that will yield useful information. A recent study by researchers at Harvard confirmed what setter people have known all along: that dogs have an uncanny ability to pick up on human gestures—even those as subtle as a glance—and accurately infer their meaning. The researchers also found that this ability is much more highly developed in dogs than in wolves, the conclusion being that humans have selected for this quality (consciously or not) in the 15,000 years or so since the dog was first domesticated. Be that as it may, if you find a puppy that can't keep its eyes off you—and especially one that's eager to meet your gaze—write the check as fast as you can.

LEATHER IS IRRESISTIBLY ATTRACTIVE to puppies, who are initially drawn to the scent and then discover, to their delight, that it feels awfully good in their mouths, too. Some trainers, in fact, swear by using an old leather glove to encourage and develop the retrieving instinct. It seems doubtful that the owner of this deck shoe intended it to be used as a retrieving dummy, however.

THESE HANDSOME, RARING-TO-GO PUPS are at that precarious but exciting age when, like human teenagers, they're starting to assert their independence—and are ready for their training to begin in earnest. You should never rush things with any pup, of course, but setters in particular require a light touch and a discerning sensibility. It's always better to err on the side of caution and apply too little pressure—even if it means progressing more slowly than you'd like—rather than too much.

ALL REPUTABLE BREEDERS take pains to socialize their puppies, handling them, playing with them, and simply exposing them to as much human contact as possible. The degree of socialization a pup receives, particularly in the first seven weeks of its life, has a direct bearing on how well—or how poorly—it takes to training. Judging by this pup's relaxed demeanor, it feels about as comfortable in the company of people as it does in the company of its littermates.

PERHAPS NO PHASE OF TRAINING demands more judgment and sensitivity than steadying a young dog—teaching it not to break once it's established point but to staunchly hold and allow its handler to flush the birds. A very bold, fiery dog can withstand a fair amount of correction without losing any style or intensity, but a dog that's on the nervous, shy, or high-strung side has to be handled with kid gloves. Forcing the issue with such a dog can lead to flagging—waving its tail on point rather than keeping it still—or, even worse, blinking: purposely avoiding birds.

GO SLOWLY, BE IMMENSELY PATIENT, rely as much as possible on praise and as little as possible on discipline, allow the marvelous natural qualities bred into the English setter to emerge and flower, and this is the reward: a dog that points staunchly, stylishly, and with terrific conviction. If you want to congratulate yourself for a job well done, go right ahead. You deserve it—although if you're smart you'll give the lion's share of the credit to your dog.

WHEN THE EFFORT to bring back the hunting Irish setter began in earnest some fifty years ago, one of the first orders of business was to produce dogs with the kind of high-tailed style on point displayed by pointers and English setters. A Pennsylvania sportsman named W. E. "Ned" LeGrande took it upon himself to locate high-tailed Irish that could serve as foundation stock, and after combing the entire United States and following up countless leads, he found one—repeat, *one*. Fortunately, Askew's Carolina Lady proved to be the right one, unfailingly passing her proud tail carriage, along with many other fine qualities, to her progeny. Today, Lady is considered the fountainhead of the modern field-bred Irish setter—and her descendants, like this strapping fellow, have style to burn.

THE IRISH SETTER, like its English counterpart, has proven its utility on every upland game bird and in every upland hunting situation North America has to offer. In fact, a good argument can be made that the overall quality of the breed is better than ever; its partisans go so far as to claim that, dog-for-dog, the red setters are superior to the white ones. And yet, they remain something of a rarity. Why the hunting Irish haven't caught on in a bigger way is one of those imponderable questions that even the breed's fans are hard-pressed to explain.

WHILE THE DOG IN THE BACKGROUND has the rich mahogany coat and robust conformation that most people associate with the breed—what you might call the Big Red stereotype—many field-bred Irish, like the dog in the foreground, are smaller, finer-boned, and more fawn or russet colored. This is the result of Field Dog Stud Book–sanctioned outcrosses in the early 1950s to white-and-orange English setters. (Askew's Carolina Lady notwithstanding, there simply weren't enough outstanding Irish setter gun dogs left to assemble a sufficiently large nucleus of breeding stock.) Partly in recognition of these crosses and partly from a desire to differentiate their dogs from the nonhunting, show-type Irish, the gun dog camp took to calling their dogs red setters. The name stuck, and today, when you hear somebody talking about red setters, you can be sure he or she is referring to the FDSB-registered field-type Irish.

WHITE MARKINGS, usually on the muzzle, chest, paws, and tail, are another legacy of the red setter's infusion of English setter blood. The interesting thing is that, according to historical accounts and pictorial representations, the original Irish setters—the setters of Ireland, that is—were themselves typically red and white, or, in dog jargon, parti-colored. It was not until the late-nineteenth century, in fact, that the solid red variety—self-colored, to use another bit of jargon—became the standard.

SETTERS, IRISH OR OTHERWISE, are no different from the rest of the canine race: They look with their eyes, but they see with their noses. As long as they're able to get a whiff of outside air, the world around them is as plain as day.

AMERICA'S FIRST IMPORTANT native-born dog artist, John M. Tracy, was
intimately familiar with all the outstanding pointers and English setters
of the late-nineteenth century. Not only did he paint them, he also hunted
over them and judged them in field trial competition. But until the end of
his life, which came prematurely in 1893 at the age of forty-nine, the Irish
setter held a special place in Tracy's affections. "The very best field dog I ever
saw was an Irish setter," he once wrote. "For those who shoot a great deal,
and work the same dog on a variety of game, there is no dog like a good
Irish setter." There are those who would stand by that statement today.

WITH ITS GLOSSY BLACK COAT trimmed in rich tan, the Gordon is arguably the handsomest setter of them all. While not as fast or wide-ranging as its English and Irish counterparts (although there are individual exceptions to this rule), its all-day stamina, superior nose, and keen desire to please make it an eminently practical gun dog, especially for ruffed grouse, woodcock, pheasant, and other birds typically found in heavier cover. Another selling point is that many Gordons are natural retrievers.

AS A BREED, the Gordon tends to be somewhat lower-tailed on point than the English or Irish setters—although, again, there are exceptions. This gives the Gordon a certain old-timey appearance, reminiscent of the depictions of the breed seen in nineteenth- and early-twentieth-century paintings. Some traditionalists even prefer the tail held at back level or just slightly above. Ultimately, though, it's what's up front—nose, brains, desire, etc.—that counts.

GORDONS ARE KNOWN for their engaging—even clownish—personalities. They seem to take a well-rounded, well-adjusted approach to life: Yes, hunting may be the most important thing— but it's not the *only* thing.

SETTERS IN GENERAL—and Gordon setters in particular—require a close relationship with their owner-handlers. The Gordon is a one-person dog through and through, the kind that expect devotion to be repaid in kind and will comprehensively ignore anybody else who tries to buddy up to it. If you think of a bird dog as a means to an end—a necessary tool of the hunt, if you will, like a shotgun—the Gordon is emphatically not the breed for you.

ONE OF THE RAPS on Gordons over the years has been that, even by setter standards, they're notoriously slow to mature. In response to this, some Gordon breeders have strived to develop more precocious strains. If this eight-week-old puppy is emblematic of her bloodline, she's definitely inherited the right stuff.

THIS IS WHEN it all comes together, the generations of breeding, the years of training, the forging of that adamant bond. It begins with the blood, as it does for all pointing breeds— but with setters blood alone is not enough. There has to something more, and that something is trust: complete, unshakable, unqualified trust. When a setter has that, it will go to the very ends of the earth, even to hell and back, to make its owner proud.

SUCH STATEMENTS are always open to question—and invariably controversial—but setter people seem to lavish more affection on their dogs than the owners of other pointing breeds. Of course, it's a two-way street, and it's the rare setter that doesn't give as good as it gets.

THE SETTERS ARE OFTEN referred to as the gentleman's gun dogs. True or not, it's certainly the case that people who hunt with setters place a premium on the aesthetics of the experience; they'd rather shoot one bird over a statuesque point than five that flush of their own accord. Setters are as productive as any other pointing dog in terms of helping you put birds in your coat, but to most setter people it's not about limiting out. It's about doing it right.

IF YOU MIND MUDDY PAWPRINTS on your pants—or if you're reluctant to rub a wet, gritty ear—you are, by definition, not a setter person.

IN HIS BOOK *English Dogges*, published in 1570, Dr. Johannes Caius provides one of the earliest descriptions of a setter at work. Noting that the name setter is "both consonant and agreeable with his quality," Caius writes that they "be serviceable for fowling, making no noise either with tongue or foot whilst they follow the game. These attend diligently upon their masters, and frame their conditions to such becks, motions and gestures as it shall please him to exhibit, inclining to the right hand or yielding to the left. . . . When he hath found the bird he keepeth sure and fast silence, and stayeth his steps, and will proceed no farther. . . ." Over four hundred years later, the setter is prized for precisely the same qualities that occasioned Caius's approbation—with an added measure of style to boot.

WITH A WORK ETHIC SECOND-TO-NONE, the German shorthaired pointer is the ultimate blue-collar bird dog, the kind that never calls in sick, always puts in an honest day's labor, and, no matter what the job, efficiently and unfussily gets it done. The shorthair is the pickup truck of pointing breeds: not flashy, perhaps, but as ruggedly and consistently reliable as they come.

In other words, it's a dog for tough-minded pragmatists who value substance over style.

The German shorthair is about as low-maintenance as a pointing dog can get, too. It doesn't require a lot of coddling, coaching, or fine-tuning; once trained, the shorthair tends to stay that way. It knows its role, and sticks to the script. Give it a little preseason conditioning, and the typical GSP is ready to pick up—no pun intended—right where it left off: hunting to the gun at medium range and moderate pace, handling easily, pointing staunchly, retrieving promptly—and screwing up very, very rarely. It's for good reason that the German shorthair is the breed of choice at shooting preserves, where the dogs, like physicians, are first required to do no harm. It's also for good reason that, among the pointing breeds whose primary registry is the American Kennel Club, the GSP leads the pack by a comfortable margin.

The German
Shorthaired Pointer

THE GERMAN SHORTHAIRED POINTER was one of the first two continental breeds—so called because they were developed on the European mainland rather than the British Isles—to gain a significant following in the United States. (The other pioneering continental was the Brittany.) A trickle of importations began in the 1920s, and the breed caught on quickly with sportsmen desiring a tractable, close-working, even-tempered dog that retrieved naturally and could maintain its easygoing pace all day long. And while Midwestern pheasant hunters have always been the shorthair's core constituency, the dog is an increasingly popular choice among those who pursue desert quail, chukar partridge, and other Western game birds.

IN ITS COUNTRY OF ORIGIN, the German shorthair—*Deutsch kurzhaar*, in the native tongue—has always been an all-purpose hunting dog, expected not only to find and point upland game birds but to help bring to bag whatever furred or feathered bounty the earth provides. As opposed to the catholicity of taste displayed by German sportsmen, however, American sportsmen tend to be more specialized, and as a result relatively few take advantage of the shorthair's versatility. Those who do know that such tasks as retrieving a goose—virtually unheard of among a lot of pointing breeds—are child's play for the GSP.

OVER THE YEARS, an Americanized version of the German shorthair has emerged that's leggier and more streamlined in appearance and, as you'd expect, faster and bigger running in the field. Some of these speed-merchant GSPs, in fact, are capable of giving the pointers and setters a run for their money. Still, many breeders continue to hew to the old standard, their ideal a dog much like this one: strong and sturdily built, with a broad skull, long, almost hound-like ears, the physical tools to perform a variety of functions, and, last but not least, the no-nonsense attitude befitting a true professional.

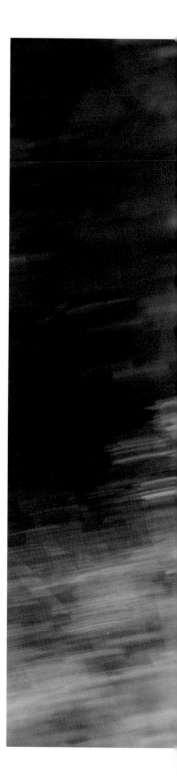

THE GERMAN SHORTHAIR is surprisingly weatherproof, capable of withstanding colder temperatures and wetter conditions than its name and
appearance might lead you to believe. Although short, obviously, the GSP's
coat affords enviable protection, with a stiff, water- and briar-repellent
outer layer and a dense undercoat for thermal insulation. Think of it as
the canine equivalent of polypropylene long underwear and a waxed
cotton coat.

ALTHOUGH AS A RULE it doesn't run with the effortless grace of the best pointers and English setters, the German shorthair is attractively gaited nevertheless, its powerful hindquarters propelling it over the ground at an easy, all-day canter, its stub tail—traditionally docked at one-third (or less) of full length but now often left at one-half—a blur of perpetual motion.

THE GSPs MODERATE RANGE, thorough pattern, and general biddability make it an excellent choice for ruffed grouse and woodcock. Still, it's never become more than mildly popular as a cover dog. Tradition, which grouse and woodcock hunters embrace to a greater degree than other shotgun-toting sportsmen, explains this in part, as the traditional choices for these birds are first the English setter and next the pointer. Another frequently voiced knock on the shorthair is that its heavy liver markings can make it difficult to locate on point—although the modern beeper collar would seem to have rendered this argument largely moot.

ONE LOOK AT THIS shorthair's face tells you that he's no stranger to brush, briars, thorns, thickets—the whole murderer's row of nasty stuff that game birds seek cover in. One look also tells you that, in typical GSP fashion, he's as diligent, tenacious, and just plain *serious* a hunting dog as you'll find anywhere.

Judging from the vegetation, this solid liver shorthair could be pointing any of several species of game birds. The smart money, though, is on pheasant—the bird that, more than any other, is associated with the GSP. It's no accident that the German shorthair became firmly established in the United States at the same time that the pheasant—also an import—was enjoying a population explosion here. Partly because of the nature of pheasant cover and partly because of the unpredictable nature of the bird itself, many hunters found the cautious, closer-working GSP a better choice than the wider-ranging pointer and English setter, which at the time (ca. 1930s-40s) were essentially the only pointing breeds available to American sportsmen. This fueled the shorthair's popularity, and although these days it's apt to be encountered anywhere, the traditional pheasant range of the upper Midwest remains its stronghold.

THE GERMAN SHORTHAIRED POINTER is often recommended as an ideal first pointing dog for the neophyte bird hunter. And with good reason: Given some basic obedience training, a thorough acclimation to gunfire, and a modicum of exposure to game, the typical GSP will turn in a creditable performance. Plus, as alluded to previously, it's about as low-maintenance as the pointing breeds get. The interesting thing is a lot of veteran hunters will tell you they like German shorthairs for the very same reasons.

DESCENDED AS THEY ARE from stoic Teutonic stock, German shorthairs aren't normally fools for love. If anything, they tend to be a bit ascetic in outlook and temperament, asking little of their owners beyond food, water, shelter, and the chance to exercise their birthright, fulfill their genetic destiny, and *go hunting*. Even a tough, hard-bitten GSP, however, likes a little reassurance now and then.

BY DINT OF THE WIDE OPEN SPACES they inhabit, the conventional wisdom is that Hungarian partridge are best hunted with pointers, English setters, or certain big-running lines of Brittanies. Clearly, this shorthair—and, more importantly, her owner—have their own thoughts on the matter. It comes back—as it usually does with German shorthairs—to versatility.

WITH AGE, the German shorthair's rich liver muzzle goes a pewtery silver-gray, lending it an air of distinguished seniority. And, for a time at least, guile and wisdom are able to compensate for the inevitable diminution of physical ability. Resting the old bones helps, too.

THE TECHNICAL TERM for the portion of a dog's ear that hangs down is the leather. (You can't say you didn't learn *something* from reading this book.) Because German shorthairs have more leather than just about any other pointing breed, their ears are scratched, rubbed, pulled, and otherwise manhandled on a regular basis. As for whether this shorthair wears an expression of enraptured bliss or one of tolerant resignation, draw your own conclusions.

As the novelist and sportsman Jim Harrison has observed, dogs are always happiest when they're doing what they've been bred to do, whether it's pulling a load, herding a flock, or pointing birds. Its all-business reputation notwithstanding, the German shorthair is no exception to this rule. A shorthair bounding through the frost-browned grass, ears flapping and eyes afire, comes dangerously close to defining exuberance. You might call it the breed's little secret.

ALTHOUGH SOME EROSION of retrieving instinct has been noted as American breeders have prioritized other abilities, retrieving still comes naturally to most German shorthairs. A GSP pup that starts out play-fetching a sock, glove, or tennis ball—an activity that's as much fun for the pup as it is for its owner—is likely to need very little formal training to become a reliable retriever of game.

THE GERMAN SHORTHAIR is among the most precocious of pointing dogs, as this seven-week-old puppy demonstrates. To watch a pup this young tighten up on point is to witness a transformation, not only from unharnessed kinetic energy to barely breathing immobility, but from carefree, what-me-worry? puppyhood to a vision of the intensely focused adult it will one day become. It's startling the way the face of a puppy on point turns into a mask of mature concentration.

A COMMON MISTAKE made by first-time puppy owners (also parents) is overthinking—and therefore over-controlling their pups' lives, as if every move the pup is allowed to make, or is prevented from making, will have dire consequences down the line. Don't fall into this trap! It's impossible to be too emphatic about how important it is to simply let your pup be a pup for awhile, affording it the opportunity to do all the silly, goofy, endearing things pups do. There'll be plenty of time later on for the serious stuff.

THE ALERT, INTELLIGENT EYES, the cocked ears, the furrowed brow: If there's a quintessential German shorthaired pointer expression, this is it. Anyone who knows German shorthairs will tell you that this pup's a keeper.

WHILE IT'S TRUE that the German shorthair tends to be an independent, tough-minded sort, it's by no stretch of the imagination an automaton. An innate desire to please is part of the makeup of all dogs—it's why they forsook the pack and went domestic in the first place—and for any relationship to succeed there has to be an element of reciprocity. There has to be trust, respect, and understanding, too, and the earlier you plant the seeds, the more vigorously and robustly they'll grow.

WHY THE BELLS? Well, for one thing, they help the pup become accustomed to noises in general; some breeders even suspend bells over their puppy pens, adjusting the height so that the pups can just bat them with their paws enough to start them ringing. It's also likely that this owner makes a habit of belling his dogs to keep track of them in heavy cover and is indoctrinating his pup at an early age.

SUCH STATEMENTS are always subject to debate, but when it comes to easily trained pointing breeds, the German shorthair is near the top of the list. Shorthairs can be stubborn and hard-headed, certainly. By and large, though, they won't fight your authority the way some breeds will; show them what's expected of them, reward them when they do it right, correct them when they don't, and they'll usually comply. They'll usually do it happily, too. That's another thing about German shorthairs: They're not sulkers; they don't hold a grudge when there's a divergence of opinion and they're made to obey the law of the land.

IT'S ONLY NATURAL, when you acquire a pointing dog puppy, to look forward to the day when the dream is finally fulfilled, and the two of you take to the field as full and equal partners in the hunt. But while you should always keep this goal in sight, don't become so pre-occupied that you forget to smell the roses along the way and enjoy the simple pleasures of puppyhood. This is one of those rare instances in which getting there really *is* half the fun—or should be.

AT THE RISK OF GILDING THE
lily, the shorthair's trainability
extends to its propensity to *stay*
trained. Once you've established
staunchness on point, for example—as exemplified by this intense
stand—you'll be able to count the
number of times the dog breaks
during the rest of its career on one
hand, probably with fingers to
spare. Shorthairs aren't perfect,
but—reflecting their German
heritage, perhaps—they do tend
to be perfectionists.

THE GERMAN SHORTHAIR'S typical m.o. when making game is to approach its birds carefully
and, if it errs at all, to err on the side of caution. In other words, you'll rarely see a shorthair
that's working scent crowd its birds and thereby cause them to flush wild. This is perhaps the
single biggest reason that the GSP enjoys such renown as a pheasant dog: Where less patient,
higher-revving breeds are brought to ruin by the ringneck's propensity to run—you can literally see them crack under the strain of repeated unproductive points—the shorthair keeps its
distance (and its cool) until the bird finds itself in a spot where holding tight seems the better
alternative. Of course, the person carrying the shotgun may suffer a nervous breakdown before
this moment of truth is reached, but that's not the dog's problem.

IF THERE'S ONE THING German shorthairs don't get enough credit for, it's their athleticism. Their steady, workmanlike manner belies a marvelous set of physical skills, including eye-opening agility and, when they need it, a surprising turn of speed. They're excellent swimmers as well, although, again, they're infrequently called upon to use this ability.

A NUMBER OF AMERICAN breeders have made it their mission to produce German shorthairs much like this: a racier, longer-legged, predominantly white dog with the drive, desire, and physical wherewithal to cover sizable chunks of country—and to cover them in a hurry. Some of these GSPs have even shown well in horseback field trial competition against pointers and English setters. It may go by the same name, but this sure ain't your daddy's German shorthaired pointer.

WHILE THE GERMAN SHORTHAIR appeals to a broad spectrum of sportsmen, the fact of the matter is that you don't see a lot of GSPs in the ownership of guys who haven't paid their dues—or aren't willing to. Shorthair people aren't wannabes or poseurs; they, like their dogs, are the Real Deal, the kind who arrive early, stay late, go the extra mile, and take their bird hunting very, very seriously.

EVEN IF YOU KNEW NOTHING about dogs, or birds, or hunting, you would know, beyond a shadow of a doubt, that this dog means business. And if you *did* know a little something about these subjects, you'd bet the bank that the birds are right where the dog says they are. An authoritative aura emanates from a German shorthair on point, especially one as proudly and upstandingly handsome as this fellow.

THE BRITTANY DOESN'T LOOK THE WAY MOST people expect a hunting dog to look. It looks, instead, like a spotted, stub-tailed, silky-coated, somewhat overgrown, perhaps even a bit roly-poly lap dog.

Nor does the Brittany behave the way most people expect a hunting dog to behave. It seems to wear a friendly (if not slightly goofy) grin 24/7, its every move exuding a breezy, happy-go-lucky nonchalance and carefree *joie de vivre* squarely at odds with the brisk, dignified carriage and steely-eyed reserve that, in the popular imagination, the rigors of the field demand.

But this is one book that can't be judged by its cover—although a lot of Brittany owners take a perverse glee in playing on the stereotype, copping an "Aw, shucks" attitude about their "fuzzy little dogs" and basically sandbagging the hell out of anyone who's uninformed, inexperienced, or just plain gullible enough to buy it. More than a few members of the pointer–setter camp, in particular, after watching a Brittany outrun, outhustle, outbird, and outlast the dogs with the long tails, had to go back and try to find the place where they dropped their jaws. They needed them to chew all that crow they had to eat.

And just so everybody's clear on this, the breed's official name these days is, simply, Brittany, not Brittany spaniel (which is how it was formerly known). The spaniel designation was dropped in the early 1980s in an effort to distinguish—and distance—the Brittany from the flushing spaniels, such as the springer and cocker. Old habits die hard, though, and the term Brittany spaniel is still part of the bird dog vernacular.

The Brittany

THE BRITTANY, along with the German shorthaired pointer, was a pioneer in establishing the continental breeds as legitimate choices for American upland bird hunting. (Continental refers to the breeds that originated on the European mainland as opposed to the British Isles.) Named for the region in northwestern France where it was developed, the Brittany was first imported to the United States in 1912, but it was not until the 1930s that the breed began to have an appreciable presence here. At that time, many American sportsmen felt that the pointer and English setter—then essentially the only pointing breeds available in this country—were too wide-ranging, headstrong, and difficult to train and control. The industrious but tractable Brittany proved to be just the kind of comfortable gunning companion these hunters were looking for, and its popularity soared as a result.

WHILE IN ITS NATIVE FRANCE the Brittany was expected to point and retrieve all manner of game for the gun—one early commentator remarked on its proficiency as a hunter of hares— in America the breed has largely evolved into an upland bird specialist. Within this specialty, however, the Brittany is remarkably versatile. Whether hunting Huns and sharptails on the high plains, pheasants in the Midwestern farm country, or ruffed grouse and woodcock in the northern forests, the Brittany has shown that it can adapt—and that it can excel. In fact, about the only part of the country where the Brittany remains something of a rarity is the "quail belt" of the Deep South, but this is more a function of the force of tradition than of any shortcomings on the dog's part.

THE BRITTANY HAS ALWAYS BEEN the gun dog of Everyman, the unpretentious, hail-fellow-well-met hunter who wants a reliable, easily handled, day in, day out companion in the field. Indeed, the Brittany was originally developed by just such men as this, not the sundry nobles, aristocrats, and landed gentry from whose kennels the other pointing breeds emerged. It was, in short, a peasant's dog—and, according to some sources, a poacher's dog. Not looking the way a hunting dog is supposed to look (see the beginning of this chapter), it aroused little suspicion among authorities. Plus, its small size helped facilitate a quick and stealthy getaway when, for example, the count's gamekeeper showed up unexpectedly.

THE BRITTANY'S SHORT-COUPLED CONFORMATION and front-to-back slope—it's typically taller at the shoulders than at the rump—give the breed a distinctive gait, a gait that's almost piston-like in its rapid cycling, controlled power, and economy of motion. And while not renowned as a speed merchant, the Britt is what you might call sneaky fast, capable of covering surprisingly large amounts of country in surprisingly short periods of time. Even more telling, though, is the way the Brittany is able to maintain a good, steady clip for hours on end. This is a dog made for the long haul.

WHILE ITS PRECISE ORIGINS are difficult to pin down—as they are for most pointing breeds—
the Brittany is believed to derive mainly from crosses between indigenous French flushing
spaniels and various types of setters, although it seems likely that a little pointer blood was
added along the way, too. In any event, by the late-1800s the Brittany had become very much
what it remains today: a dog that points with confidence and intensity, standing off its birds
at a respectful distance but locating them positively and accurately. This brings up another of
the breed's acknowledged strengths: an unusually keen nose.

THIS STAUNCHLY POINTING BRITTANY displays the classic hallmarks of the breed: compact size; moderate feathering; high-set ears; short, slightly tapered muzzle; gracefully sloping profile; an overall impression of alert intelligence and bouncy athleticism. The stub tail is another signature. The Brittany is unique among the continental breeds in that it is often born with such a tail—what you might call naturally docked. Some Britts, in fact, are virtually tailless at birth. Longer tails—which also occur—are docked to conform to the breed standard of four inches or less.

THE SHARP-TAILED GROUSE poses several challenges for a pointing dog. The coveys are often found in thin cover—stubble fields and short-grass prairie, for example—where they can see danger coming a long way off and as a result are likely to flush without giving dog or gunner a chance. And even if the dog does have an opportunity to work them, the birds may simply refuse to hold. Then, once they scatter, a different problem arises: For reasons that aren't entirely clear, single sharptails seem to emit less scent (especially considering their size) than just about any other game bird. Locating these needles in a haystack requires a dog with a keen nose and a busy style of hunting—qualities that the Brittany has in abundance.

EXPERIENCED HUNTERS DON'T EXPECT their dogs to remain staunch when the birds have run and the dog is pointing where they were. Instead, savvy hunters rely on their dogs to stay in contact with running birds, relocating on their own recognizance and carefully but determinedly following the thread of scent until the birds find themselves in a spot where holding tight seems the safer alternative. This high-wire act goes by several names: roading, the moving point, the serial relocation, among others. By any name, the Brittany, with its perfectly proportioned mix of dash and caution, is a master at it.

THE RING-NECKED PHEASANT, a Eurasian import
that by the 1930s had become well established from
California to New York, helped set the stage for the
Brittany's arrival here. As noted elsewhere, many
American sportsmen were generally dissatisfied
with the big-running pointers and English setters
of the day. The frustration of hunting running,
wild-flushing pheasants with these horizon-busters
brought this dissatisfaction to a head—and opened
the door for continental breeds such as the Brittany,
which were closer working, easier to handle, and
simply more pleasant to gun over.

MOST BRITTANIES WILL NATURALLY honor another dog's point. But then, there isn't much that the typical Brittany, given the proper exposure, experience, and encouragement, won't do— or figure out—on its own. This high level of instinctive ability, coupled with the breed's terrific eagerness-to-please, makes it one of the best choices for the first-time pointing dog owner.

THE HUNGARIAN PARTRIDGE is a notorious runner, surpassed in this respect among North American game birds only by the pheasant (although the scaled quail also has its partisans). Huns are also famous—or maybe infamous—for being unusually difficult to anchor, i.e., to bring down in such a conclusive way that they *stay* down. A Hun with even a breath of life will use it to run as far as it can or tuck into some pocket of heavy cover in an effort to avoid detection. That the Brittany shines as a Hun dog is a testament to its ability not only to handle them properly and therefore produce them for the gun, but to bring the fugitives to justice.

WHILE THE BRITTANY isn't the water retriever that some of the continental breeds are—its coat, like that of the setters, tends to absorb water rather than shed it—it's the rare Britt that hesitates to take the plunge when there's a bird on the line. Most Brittanies, in fact, love to swim. Most are very good at it, too.

YES, THESE ARE BRITTANIES; no, they're not the Brittanies you're probably familiar with. They are, to be precise, French Brittanies. Strictly speaking, of course, the term is redundant—it's something like saying Canadian Manitobans—but it is used specifically to distinguish Brittanies imported from France in the past twenty to twenty-five years (or their direct descendants) from the lines of Brittanies developed by American breeders. The French Brittany is typically smaller than its American counterpart, and while the American standard allows no color combinations other than white and orange (by far the most prevalent here) or white and liver, the French dogs come in a veritable rainbow of hues, including white and black; white, black, and tan (tricolored); liver roan; the list goes on. Dark noses and eyes are other identifying characteristics of the French Brittany.

IRONICALLY, GIVEN THE ROLE that discontent with the status quo played in bringing the Brittany to popularity on this side of the pond, the French Brittany owes its presence here to sportsmen who found themselves in much the same boat. Their contention was that American breeders, dazzled by the allure of horseback field trial competition (and the prospect of beating the pointers and English setters at their own game), had played fast and loose with the Brittany's heritage and in the process created a dog very different from the original Brittany type: larger, leggier, and, in particular, much wider ranging. The biddable, close-working, compact kind of Brittany prized by shoe-leather bird hunters, they argued, had become almost impossible to find in the United States. So, returning to the source, they looked to France, where the traditional, old-style Brittany remained de rigueur.

ROAN, AS DISPLAYED BY this liver roan French Brittany, is created by a fine mixture of colored hairs with white ones. While orange and liver roans are occasionally seen in American lines (and are acceptable under the American breed standard), roans in general are much more common among the French dogs. The variety known as blue roan, by the way, is something of an optical illusion: The colored hairs are actually black.

IN TERMS OF PERFORMANCE, the most significant way in which the French Brittany differs from its American cousin is that it typically hunts at much closer range. Whether you view this as an asset or a liability is largely a matter of personal preference, and, in the interest of full disclosure, there are a lot of Brittany people in this country who believe the French Brittany represents not an improvement, but a step backwards. Philosophical questions aside, however, at the most fundamental level a Brittany is a Brittany—which is to say, an attentive, indefatigable little bird-finding machine.

AT FIRST GLANCE, you'd almost mistake this French Brittany for a Gordon setter. Or, if you're exceptionally knowledgeable about sporting dogs, an English hunting cocker—perhaps the only other member of the sporting group, in fact, that comes in as many color combinations.

ONE QUALITY THAT ALL Brittanies have in common is that they're emphatically *people* dogs. They want to be your buddy—if not your best friend—and they'll go to shameless lengths to ingratiate themselves. If you're uncomfortable with public displays of affection, the Brittany is not the breed for you.

AMONG THE THINGS that every sportsman should do before checking out is raise a litter of puppies. It's just such a rewarding experience, from the excitement of planning the breeding to the anticipation of the litter's arrival to the day the fist-sized puppies enter the world—and then the fun *really* begins. Truth to tell, though, for the first three or four weeks after the pups are whelped, your role is largely that of an observer. Assuming the dam's maternal instincts are sound—as is clearly the case with this serene Brittany, a brood matron par excellence—Mama does just about all the work. But once the weaning process starts . . . well, you'd best be prepared for some sleepless nights—or at least some early wake-up calls.

EVERY LITTER HAS its pecking order, its pups that are shyer and more submissive, its pups that are bolder and more aggressive. Assuming a pup doesn't display unusual tendencies toward one end of the spectrum or the other, however—the pup that's afraid of its own shadow, for example—there's every likelihood that it will develop into a well-adjusted, well-mannered family member, hunting companion, and canine citizen. The key—broken-record time again—is doing your homework and finding a litter with the right genetic stuff. Beyond that, you're just splitting hairs.

IT'S NEVER TOO EARLY to begin bonding with a puppy—and there's no such thing as spending too much time with a pup, especially when it's acclimating to its new home and family. You have to remember that a weanling puppy's entire world has been comprised of its dam, its littermates, its whelping box, a handful of people—and not a heck of a lot else. So, when a pup is removed from everything that's familiar to it, there's bound to be some emotional trauma involved. It's up to you to make the transition as stress-free as possible. The good news is that if you start with a well-bred, well-socialized puppy—a category that includes the vast majority of Brittanies—chances are that it'll take to you and yours like a duck to water.

WHETHER YOU BELIEVE it has legitimate value or not, you have to admit that teasing a puppy into pointing a wing is a heck of a lot of fun. Some pups will lock up instantaneously when a wing is flicked in front of them; others will try to pounce on it a time or two (or three or four), only styling up on point when it becomes apparent that the Pickett's Charge approach isn't working and that stealthier tactics are indicated. The wing game *is* a game, to be sure, but as long as you play it sparingly it's hard to see that it does any harm—especially when all the parties to it so obviously enjoy themselves.

YOU NEVER WANT TO PUSH a pup this young to be staunch on point. In fact, a lot of trainers actually prefer that pups this age break and chase, arguing that it increases their boldness and confidence, and that once they've learned they can't catch the birds the staunching process becomes that much easier. But if you're blessed with a pup that's *naturally* staunch, there's nothing wrong with gently encouraging and reinforcing the behavior. And it's always a good sign when a pointing pup will let you put your hands on it without wilting—that is, without losing any style, intensity, or rigidity. All else equal, it augurs for smooth sailing later on, when the serious training starts.

THE WAY THIS PUP has reflexed onto point bodes well for her future—and for the future of those lucky enough to gun over her. In real-world bird hunting, dogs don't always have the option of stretching out in a classic full-body point when they catch scent; sometimes they have to freeze *now*, midstride, because one more step could spell the disaster of bumped birds and a wild flush. Not every dog has the sheer athletic ability to pull this off. Those that do—and this pretty pup appears well on her way—are the ones that have the chance to become something special.

PUPPIES WILL BE PUPPIES—and, within reasonable limits, puppy owners should let them. It's tempting to speculate that this pup, having committed some major indiscretion—the mind reels at the possibilities—is proffering the equivalent of an olive branch. But in all likelihood it's just having fun, its interior monologue going something like "I have a really cool branch—and you don't. Hah!"

BELYING THEIR LONG COATS, Brittanies as a rule are fairly tolerant of hot, dry conditions. This is one of the reasons the breed enjoys such a large and loyal following in places such as Montana—where temperatures early in the season can be brutal—and the Southwest. Tolerant, however, is not the same as impervious, so when water becomes available over the course of a day's hunt you should let your dog take advantage of it, even if it requires a little detour. In parts of the West, a stock tank may offer the only water for miles around.

THE GLEAM IN THIS PUP'S EYE speaks to its intelligence and, judging by the intensity with which the pup is staring at whatever's grabbed its attention, its ability to focus. Both of these qualities will serve it well in the years to come.

THE BRITTANY IS A HIGHLY refined, highly sophisticated creation, the product of countless generations of selective breeding. But it's still a dog—and there hasn't been one yet that wouldn't try to cadge a piece of a bird hunter's sandwich. Oh, and if this particular bird hunter looks familiar, it's because he's the well-known writer, shotgun authority, and bon vivant Michael McIntosh.

BIRD HUNTERS SERIOUS ENOUGH about their sport to pull dog trailers—which aren't cheap, by the way—are unlikely to fill them with potlickers. They have too much at stake to trust their fortunes afield to mediocre dog flesh: too much time, too much money, too much emotional capital invested to hazard a skimpy payoff. This is why, when you see a dog trailer, you can take it to the bank that its cargo—like this leggy, deep-chested Brittany—is several cuts above average. As a bumper sticker popular among field trialers says, "If you can't run with the big dogs, stay on the porch."

THE BRITTANY'S COAT does require a certain amount of maintenance, although in normal circumstances they do an amazingly thorough job of self de-burring. Every so often, however, they'll inadvertently wander into a patch of cockleburs and come out looking like their feathers have been braided into cornrows. What looked good on Bo Derek looks ugly on a Brittany—not to mention the irritation it causes to the dog's skin and the hindrance it can prove to movement—so when this happens it's time to dig the steel comb out of the gear bag and get to work. While there's bound to be an occasional whine of protest when hair in sensitive areas is pulled, Brittanies in general submit to these sessions with stoic tolerance. Then, when the job is done, they get up, shake themselves briskly, and become their ebullient selves once again.

AS A RULE, SNOW doesn't bother Brittanies much. If anything, they welcome the white stuff. There's a limit, though, to how much snow and cold a body can stand, and it's pretty clear that this Britt's getting close to it. A plane ticket to St. Bart's not being in the cards, a brisk rub with a dry towel—which astute hunters always carry several of—and a warm kennel to curl up in will probably have to do.

MAKING A BUDDY of your Brittany and spending time with it in nonhunting situations—letting it ride up front with you while you run errands, for example—is a great way to build rapport, instill trust, and develop a mutually respectful, mutually adoring relationship. Think this doesn't carry over into the field? Think again.

SOME BIRD DOGS will hunt for anyone who happens to be carrying a shotgun. But for a Brittany to give you all it's got, you have to take the time to develop a close, caring relationship. You have to forge a bond. Yes, it's important that you establish your authority as the leader of the pack, the alpha wolf, and it's important that this authority be respected. But you can't be a despot—at least not with a Brittany. Instead, you have to demonstrate that when it pleases you, good things come to it. Once a Brittany makes this connection and knows it can depend on you—lavish praise helps the process along, of course—you'll have something bigger than a relationship. You'll have a partnership.

GRANTED, THE BRITTANY'S points aren't the theatrical productions that those of some breeds are—you don't imagine sparks flying—but no breed points more intently or honestly. In fact, there's an abiding honesty at the core of everything the Brittany does—a reflection, perhaps, of the sturdy values of the people who gave the breed its identity, people who lived close to the land, worked hard for their daily bread, and took delight in small, simple pleasures. At the same time, though, the Brittany does have a certain plucky élan—and its *joie de vivre* is undeniable.

IT DOESN'T GET ANY BETTER THAN THIS: grand country, sharp-tailed grouse, and a trusted Brittany to lead the way to them. Rainbow? What rainbow?

THE VERSATILE BREEDS ARE EXACTLY WHAT the name implies: breeds developed to perform a variety of functions in addition to finding and pointing upland birds. Like the Brittany and German shorthaired pointer (which are versatiles themselves, strictly speaking), these breeds originated on the European mainland (the terms versatile and continental are essentially interchangeable) and reflect the robust enthusiasms and catholic tastes of sportsmen there, whose bags might include literally any furred or feathered game they encountered over the course of a day's hunt: partridge, duck, hare, fox, even deer. Their dogs, in turn, were expected to point what they could and roust from cover what they couldn't; to retrieve with equal aplomb from land or water; to track wounded game for as long as it took; and generally to handle whatever tasks that, by dint of their nose, speed, strength, stamina, and, if necessary, their teeth, they were better equipped to discharge than their two-legged partners.

Among American hunters, the versatiles that have achieved the greatest popularity are the German wirehaired pointer (often referred to by its German name, Drahthaar), the Weimaraner, the wirehaired pointing griffon, and the Viszla. While this doesn't exhaust the list of versatile breeds, the others—the large and small Munsterlander, the Italian spinone (which is not an ice cream flavor), the Braque d'Auvergne, the German longhaired pointer, etc.—are so rare here that many widely traveled sportsmen have never laid eyes on any of them. They have their supporters, to be sure, but what they bring to the party that the better-established versatiles don't—other than the appeal of the obscure—is hard to figure.

The Versatile Breeds

WITH ITS ROUGH COAT, rugged constitution, and diverse abilities, the German wirehaired pointer is a true all-purpose hunting dog. A strong case can be made that the wirehair (or Drahthaar, as many of its exponents prefer to call it) is the best choice for the sportsman whose primary focus is upland bird hunting and who prefers a pointing dog—but who does a significant amount of waterfowling as well. The GWP is probably the most weatherproof of all the pointing breeds, and with the addition of a neoprene vest—such as this gray-muzzled veteran is wearing—it's capable of withstanding all but the coldest and iciest conditions.

RELATED TO THE DRAHTHAAR and often mistaken for its more common cousin by the uninitiated, the wirehaired pointing griffon is a comparatively young breed—it dates only to the late-nineteenth century—and one of the few whose origin can be traced to a single individual: E. K. Korthals. Korthals, who was born in Holland but lived in Germany and, ultimately, France during the time he was developing the WPG, mingled the blood of a variety of rough-coated hunting dogs that were generically known as griffons until he produced the type he wanted: a physically stout, psychologically sound hunting companion that was capable of doing just about whatever a sportsman could ask, regardless of game, terrain, or weather.

ALTHOUGH ITS PRECISE HISTORY is disputed—as is its antiquity—the Viszla's roots are believed to lie in the game-rich Magyar Plains of Hungary and to stretch back to the pre-firearms era, when the chief task of *all* pointing breeds, as they existed then, was to locate coveys of partridge, quail, and other birds at which falconers could fly their hunting hawks. Whatever its origins, however, it's clear that the Viszla was developed primarily as a bird dog. It's typically more streamlined, more finely boned, and more graceful in action than the other versatiles, the other side of the coin being that it is somewhat less adept at tracking wounded game and less suited to water work and the rigors of cold weather.

THESE DAYS, as a result of the incredible popularity of the work of photographer William Wegman, it's hard to look at a Weimaraner and not imagine it wearing a tiara, or a fez, or one of the countless other items of apparel with which Wegman has costumed his own Weimaraners over the years before posing them for the camera. This—along with the residue of the "wonder dog" hype that prompted gullible Americans to shell out absurd amounts of money for Weimaraner pups in the 1950s (and established expectations *no* breed could live up to)—has led many sportsmen to view the "gray ghost" with a jaundiced eye. 'Tis a pity, because a Weimaraner from proven hunting stock can be an effective and enjoyable gunning companion.

ONE OF THE CRITICISMS leveled at the versatile breeds, especially by the pointer–setter camp, is that they lack intensity on point. You rarely hear this complaint directed at the German wirehair, however, which—as exemplified by this upstanding specimen—displays enough intensity and resoluteness to satisfy the most demanding judge. Yoked with the breed's tenacity, biddability, and rolling, all-day gait, it makes for a combination that many shoe-leather bird hunters will tell you is hard to beat.

THE COATS OF GERMAN WIREHAIRS exhibit considerable variation. Some, true to the breed's name, are bristly all over; others are relatively smooth, with the longer, coarser hair confined to the muzzle, ears, and eyebrows. By the same token, some wirehairs, like the lady in this photograph (no sideshow cracks, please), have pronounced beards, while in others what passes for a beard is little more than a fringe. It's easy to mistake a GWP with this kind of minimalist styling for a German shorthair, and in fact the breeds are very similar in coloration, conformation, and action.

GERMAN WIREHAIRS have a reputation for being one-man dogs—dogs whose allegiance is pledged wholly to their masters, and who treat all other humans with varying degrees of disdain, ranging from benign indiffer-ence to outright contempt. They also tend to be more protective of their turf—and what they perceive as their possessions—than other pointing breeds, and as a result can be a bit prickly toward people they're not famil-iar with. This is why it's always a good idea, when making the acquaintance of a Drahthaar, to have its owner facilitate the introduction.

ALTHOUGH THE NATURAL RANGE of the GWP is on the close to moderate side, the breed is surprisingly willing—and able—to stretch its legs in open country. And, of course, an experienced hunter will encourage his dog to do just that, loosening the handle and allowing it to ramble some. It's simple mathematics: All else equal, the more real estate your dog covers, the more birds it's going to find. A dog that adjusts its range to the character of the terrain is also displaying its intelligence, and in this arena the wirehair takes a back seat to none.

IT'S ALL BUT UNHEARD OF for a Drahthaar not to be an eager natural retriever. This is a quality that continues to be emphasized by American enthusiasts, in particular those aligned with
Verein Deutsch Drahthaar (VDD), the breed's German parent organization, rather than the
American Kennel Club. The VDD requires that all Drahthaars used for breeding pass a rigor-
ous series of ability tests—pointing, retrieving, tracking, etc.—and conformation inspections;
those that fail in any area are essentially red-flagged, meaning that the VDD will not recog-
nize their offspring. And while wirehair is the literal translation of Drahthaar, certain members of the VDD crowd insist that their dogs be referred to only by the latter—and tend to
bristle when you call them anything else.

ITS FAMOUS INTENSITY, resolve, loyalty, and seriousness of purpose notwithstanding, the Drahthaar has a definite clownish streak. But then, a dog with a face like that would have to.

MANY SPORTSMEN are of the opinion that the German wirehaired pointer is in a class by itself as a retriever of runners—poorly hit birds that fall at the shot only to hustle away on foot. Indeed, its ability in this respect is nothing short of astonishing, as time and time again it rounds up birds given up for lost (and which most other breeds simply would have stopped looking for). The bottom line is that the Drahthaar's strongly developed tracking instinct, coupled with its tenacity and patience, often spells the difference between a light game bag and a heavy one—and, at the same time, transforms a marginal wing shot into a hero.

HERE'S ONE OF THOSE WIREHAIRS that could almost pass for a German shorthair. This shouldn't be too surprising, really, for GSP blood was prominent among the crosses that helped create the Drahthaar in the late-nineteenth century, a date that makes it a comparatively recent addition to the pointing dog scene. Although immediately popular in its homeland, the wirehair was fairly slow to catch on in America; the first importations were made in the 1930s, with AKC recognition not coming until 1959. Since then, however—and especially in the last twenty years or so—the breed has established itself as one to be reckoned with. The hunter who guns a variety of birds under a variety of conditions—and is able to maintain his objectivity—has got to give the wirehair serious consideration.

TO LOOK AT THESE WIREHAIR PUPS, you'd never guess they were the same breed, much less littermates. But they are (although the fuzzier of the two could pass for a wirehaired pointing griffon, which like the German shorthair was part of the Drahthaar's original rootstock). Without wanting to make too much of it, though, such a pronounced difference in appearance ultimately makes the task of picking one pup over the other easier for the prospective owner. Many authorities hold that the overall quality of the German wirehair in this country is unsurpassed—a great tribute to its breeders and their uncompromising ethic—and when you're as certain as you are of the sun coming up that the whole litter has the right stuff, choosing a pup based on its eye appeal makes as much sense as any other method.

BEAUTY IS IN THE EYE of the beholder, but to fans of the German wirehair this goateed fellow is about as ruggedly handsome as they come. It's obvious, too—or should be—that he's not a dog to be trifled with.

ONE TRAIT THE COPPER-COATED Hungarian shares with the other versatile breeds is a strong inclination to retrieve. It's the rare Viszla that, given a little praise and encouragement, won't retrieve promptly, reliably, and tenderly to hand. The Viszla also does a better-than-average job of hunting dead game and tracking down fugitive runners. A cynic might surmise that perhaps it's no coincidence the breed bears a slight, but nevertheless undeniable, resemblance to the blood-hound—and in fact it seems highly likely that the Vis-zla's ancestry includes hounds of some type.

THE VISZLA IS SOMETHING of an anomaly among the versatile breeds. It's typically finer-boned, lighter on its feet, and more elegant in action—compelling evidence that bird hunting was (and is) its primary mission, not merely one of many jobs it was expected to do equally well. The breed's comparatively thin coat—which serves it well in hot weather but is a liability in cold, wet conditions or severely thorny cover—leads to this conclusion as well. Temperament is another area of differentiation. In dog parlance, the Viszla—again, counter to the versatile norm—is considered "soft," that is, sensitive and easily bruised. The other side of this coin is that the Viszla's gentle, affectionate nature makes it a fine choice for assuming a dual hunting dog/family dog role.

BLESSED WITH AN OUTSTANDING nose, a full measure of bird sense, and plenty of point, the great majority of Viszlas, given half a chance, will develop into top-notch hunting companions. In fact, if you simply take them afield and expose them to lots of birds, they'll usually figure out the rest on their own. What you emphatically *don't* want to do with a Viszla is employ harsh or heavy-handed training methods. It'd be like running heirloom porcelain through a car wash.

ALTHOUGH THE VISZLA is now a thriving, well-established breed, its future was far from secure in the mid-twentieth century. In fact, the Viszla was gravely imperiled then, its native Hungary having been turned upside down by two world wars and the Soviet takeover that followed the fall of Nazi Germany. Fortunately, a number of Hungarian expatriates brought their beloved dogs with them to the West, and from this seed stock the breed was able to regain its footing. The first Viszlas were imported to America in the 1950s, and the AKC granted the breed official recognition in 1960.

PUPPIES AND KIDS GO TOGETHER like milk and cookies. Having a puppy helps expand a child's emotional horizons and learn patience and responsibility; having a child helps a puppy gain confidence and become comfortable with its human family. This is especially important with a breed like the Viszla that requires a heavy dose of positive reinforcement and needs to feel that it belongs, unconditionally and without qualification. Kids have a way of pulling on things, though—puppy ears, for example—so there should always be a parent around to supervise.

THERE'S A SCHOOL OF THOUGHT that holds puppies should not be allowed to chase flushed birds, the theory being that by allowing them to chase you surrender control, tacitly encourage disobedience, and needlessly delay their development into useful gun dogs. Well, while it's true that some trainers achieve perfectly acceptable results with this approach, most authorities believe there's no harm—and often terrific value—in letting a pup be a pup, do what comes naturally, and chase birds all over creation. There'll be plenty of time later on, when the pup is physically and psychologically equipped for it, to establish control. As the esteemed professional trainer A. H. "Al" Brenneman liked to say, your top priority with puppies should be "to keep the going fiery."

A PUPPY DOING ONE OF THE JOBS its breed is supposed to do—retrieving, in this instance—wears such a serious expression, the way a kid does when he or she is charged with some important, "grown-up" task. Seeing it always brings a smile—and, you hope, a glimpse of the pleasures and satisfactions to come.

RARE—ALTHOUGH NOT, STRICTLY speaking, obscure—the wirehaired pointing griffon (the accent is on the second syllable; grif-FAWN) is apt to be mistaken for the more common Drahthaar. The griffon, however, is even shaggier in appearance than the German wirehair; if it puts you in mind of an Old English sheepdog, it's probably a griff. (Although the best way to make a positive I.D. is simply to ask—the owner, not the dog.) Many sportsmen also erroneously assume that the breed originated in Germany, but in fact the griffon's founding father, E. K. Korthals, carried out the bulk of his breeding program in France, where it continues to be known as Korthals's griffon.

WITH A BOUNCY GAIT and a hunting style best described as industrious but methodical, the wirehaired pointing griffon is perhaps the most reliably close-working dog of the established pointing breeds. A horizon-buster it ain't. This makes the griff a good choice for the wingshooter who likes to take his time and comb the cover very thoroughly—but a poor choice for the sports-man who likes to keep moving and expects his dog to gobble big chunks of real estate.

GRIFFONS ARE RETRIEVERS par excellence, not only on land but in water, where their dense coats provide ample thermal protection in all but the coldest temperatures—and in which, given the slightest opportunity, they frolic like otters. But then, griffs, as a rule, are an ebullient, fun-loving bunch of serious hunters who don't take themselves too seriously. They're definite people dogs, too. Tending to mope when confined to a kennel, griffons soak up attention like sponges and require a close, mutually adoring relationship with their owners in order to perform to the best of their considerable abilities.

THE GRIFFON'S POINTS aren't big, showy productions, the way that, say, the points of English setters and pointers tend to be. This is partly a matter of perception: Swathed in all that fur, the griff looks rather amorphous compared to the shorter-coated breeds, whose rippling musculatures lend a dramatic note to the proceedings. But for those whose idea of bird hunting doesn't include the element of spectacle, the griffon's solidly utilitarian points leave nothing to be desired. The proof, after all, is in the pudding—or in the satisfying heft of a bulging game bag.

METHODICAL DOES NOT MEAN unhappy. A griffon bounding through the cover exudes joy— the joy all dogs exude when they're doing what they're bred to do, which is the same thing as what they love to do. Dogs, unlike people, are never "conflicted" about their purpose in life.

MANY SPORTSMEN WOULD BE SURPRISED to learn that, among the pointing breeds whose primary registry is the American Kennel Club, the Weimaraner is second only to the German shorthair in number of registrations. What makes this surprising is that so few Weimaraners are encountered in bird hunting milieus, and it brings home the sobering fact that in twenty-first-century America the Weimaraner is essentially a pet breed and only marginally a working gun dog. As mentioned previously, the photographs of William Wegman have made the Weimaraner a hot commodity, even something of an arty status symbol. The upshot is that while good hunting Weimaraners can still be found, they're conspicuously in the minority. If you have your heart set on a Weimaraner as a gunning companion, take pains to do your home-work and keep the cautionary dictum *caveat emptor*—buyer beware—in mind at all times.

WITH THE EXCEPTION of the striking coat color that's earned it the nickname "gray ghost," the Weimaraner is physically, functionally, and temperamentally similar to the German shorthaired pointer. This is no coincidence, as the modern type of both breeds emerged in nineteenth-century Germany, and the development of both was directed by upper-class sportsmen who desired an all-purpose hunting dog (but who increasingly prioritized bird hunting as big game grew scarce in the late-1800s). The Weimaraner's moderate range, steady pace, businesslike demeanor in the field, and resolute attitude on point are also remindful of the GSP.

TOUTED AS A WONDER DOG by certain starry-eyed outdoor writers, the market for Weimaraners was so hot in the 1950s—and the prices so high—that unscrupulous breeders began churning out puppies simply to meet the demand. It was a lose–lose situation. In the first place, no dog made of flesh and blood could live up to the kind of outrageous hype being blithely tossed around; in the second, as the American gene pool was flooded with ill-bred pups, the overall quality of the breed inexorably declined. Knowledgeable sportsmen shunned it as a result, and the statement "I've never seen a decent Weimaraner" was repeated so often that it became a virtual cliché. Fortunately, thanks to the efforts of a few dedicated breeders, this trend shows signs of reversing—but there's still a long way to go.

ELEGANT AND REFINED, the Weimaraner's profile bespeaks intelligence, alertness, loyalty, quiet confidence, and unquestioned competence—not to mention its aristocratic roots.

THERE'S AN OLD ADAGE among gun dog people that goes something like this: While some breeds are better than others, there are good individuals within every breed. This certainly holds true of the Weimaraner. Even in the worst of times, a few gray ghosts did their forebears proud, hewing to the old standards and serving to remind the American sporting public that the breed is capable of remarkable feats. A truly accomplished Weimaraner is a pearl of great price—as those fortunate enough to own one will enthusiastically attest.

PART ART AND PART SCIENCE, BASED ON established principles but guided by intuition and judgment, training is the human half of the bird dog equation. It's what we bring to the party, what we try to alloy with our dog's instinctive, genetically inherited abilities to give them structure and focus. The goal is to allow these abilities to emerge and develop while gently shaping them to conform to our desires; to instill responsiveness and the recognition of our authority, but to retain (and encourage) all of the boldness, enthusiasm, and independence. As the eminent pointing dog authority Robert G. Wehle liked to say, the best training "leaves no fingerprints."

Or, as he expressed it in *Wing & Shot*, his classic book on gun dog training: "The actual mechanics of training are quite simple. The difficult and important part is how the mechanics are carried out and what you have left when the job is done."

And while the typical bird hunter is usually satisfied with less-than-perfect execution in this regard, the sportsman who field trials his dogs has no such option. In the crucible of competition, any shortcoming will eventually be exposed, any flaw revealed, any attempt to disguise a weakness unmasked. "Good enough" doesn't cut it; the margin for error that hunters learn to tolerate is, in the field trial realm, the kiss of death.

Oh, you might think you have a well-trained dog; you might even feel a little smug and self-congratulatory about the job you did training it. But you have no real basis for comparison until you've seen the kind of performance a field trial champion is capable of—and, in particular, the mind-boggling degree of poise and polish a champion is expected to display. It tends to be a sobering experience—but it can also provide just the motivation you need to get off your butt, get out with your dog, and take care of unfinished business.

Training and Trialing

DOZENS OF BOOKS have been written on pointing dog training; countless magazine articles have been devoted to it. But if there's one thing they all agree on, it's this: There's no substitute for simply spending time with your dog. And while this holds true for dogs of any age, it's especially important with puppies. Spending time with your pup, just getting to know one another and becoming buddies—at home, in the yard, wherever and whenever you can—lays the foundation for a lasting rapport and makes the transition to serious training as frictionless as possible. Sure, there are bound to be some rough patches—there always are—but if your relationship is built on the solid ground of mutual trust, respect, and adoration you'll find a way to get through them, together.

IT ALL STARTS WITH the pointing instinct. Everything else that a pointing dog does in the field either derives from this act or serves to support it. You don't train a dog to point, of course (although you can); instead, you encourage the instinct to emerge and provide the water, the sunlight, and the fertile soil it needs to mature and flower. In other words, you expose your pup to birds, birds, and more birds. Then, with the exception of some gentle restraint with a checkcord to help establish staunchness (if necessary), the best thing you can do is stay out of the way. The birds themselves are better teachers than you could ever hope to be.

ALL ELSE EQUAL, establishing staunchness on point—what old-time trainers called "gun dog broke"—is the single most critical passage in the education of a bird dog. Some dogs are virtually born staunch; others will test your patience to the limit in their willful insistence on breaking point and flushing the birds. This is one aspect of training in which pen-raised birds, because they allow you to control the situation, can be indispensable: You plant the bird, work your dog into it on a long checkcord (preferably at a right angle to the wind so that the dog catches scent suddenly), and then, once the dog points, ease your way up the checkcord while softly repeating the "whoa" command. Ideally, you'll have a helper along who can flush the bird for you—even if it means getting down on all fours. Comical as it looks, it's actually a good test for the dog: The more commotion it can withstand without breaking point, the closer it is to becoming reliably staunch. If you're wondering about the orange string tied to the quail, it adds just enough of a burden to cause the bird to fly only a short distance, thus allowing it to be reused, or even recaptured.

DESPITE THE MANY ADVANTAGES pen-raised birds offer for training purposes, they must be used intelligently and judiciously. As a rule, you should try to plant them in different places on your training grounds from one session to the next, and always in the kinds of places where wild birds might be found. You should also watch for signs that your dog is getting wise to the game—that is, that it's learned it can take liberties with planted birds that their wild counterparts would never permit, such as creeping on point or pointing too closely. This tells you it's time to cut back on the pen-raised stuff and, if at all possible, get your dog on wild birds. Think of it this way: You can train a dog on pen-raised birds, but you *educate* a dog on wild ones.

WHEN A DOG ON POINT lets you put your hands on it, stroking and styling it up—and, in particular, allows you to do so without losing its composure or intensity—you're well on your way to having a dog that'll stay staunch until hell freezes over. Soon it'll be time to unclip the checkcord, turn your dog loose to hunt and handle birds on its own—and find out just how good a trainer you really are.

ELECTRONIC TRAINING COLLARS—e-collars, for short—are fabulous training tools, effective and humane in the hands of those who know how and when to use them. But that's the rub: They must always be used with the utmost discretion and restraint, especially in the presence of game (when instilling staunchness on point, for example). A skilled trainer knows how to time the stimulation—a.k.a. the correction—so that the dog associates it only with its own errant behavior. An ill-timed or overly aggressive correction, on the other hand, may result in the dog's associating it with the birds—about the worst scenario possible, one that can lead to flagging on point, even outright blinking. This is why most amateur trainers, if they insist on using the e-collar, should stick to using it to correct faults. Its use as a bona fide teaching tool is better left to the pros.

MANY DOGS WILL NATURALLY honor, or back, another dog's point—and those that don't should be taught to. (If you want to become a pariah among your bird hunting friends, show up with a dog that won't honor, and instead steals point or, even worse, blows past the pointing dog and takes out the birds.) Training a dog to back—which is short for backpoint, by the way—isn't complicated. Like so many aspects of training, it's largely a matter of repetition, of providing positive reinforcement when you can—allowing the dog being taught to back to retrieve the bird, for example—and enforcing discipline when you have to. And if you don't have access to a live dog for yours to honor, a plywood cutout works just fine.

THERE'S NO MAGIC formula that tells you when it's time to remove the checkcord, although one rule of thumb states that when you think your dog's got it, you should keep up the routine for two more weeks just to be on the safe side. Judging by this setter's proud and resolute stance, however, she's ready to prove her mettle *now*.

EVERY POINTING DOG has a natural range, from close working to big running, with certain breeds and even lines of breeds displaying specific tendencies in this regard. This is one of the major factors to take into consideration when selecting the breed—and the litter—that's right for you, your style of hunting, the kinds of birds you typically hunt, and the kinds of places you typically hunt them. What you need to keep in mind, though—and many inexperienced pointing dog owners have trouble coming to grips with this—is that a pointing dog's role is to get out from underfoot and find birds *for* you. In other words, it defeats the pointing dog's purpose to demand that it hunt within gun range; to perform at its best—and to find the maximum number of birds—it needs the freedom to take the country as it comes, to be, in a very real sense, improvisational. If your dog still hunts too wide for you, though, there are a number of proven methods you can use to bring it in, such as repeatedly working it in very heavy cover, checkcording to instill handling response and pattern control, and activating the "hearing aid"—the e-collar—when your dog's range becomes excessive.

THIS TRAINER HAS PLANTED a pigeon with its wings crossed to give his dogs a point-and-honor opportunity—as well as a test of their staunchness through a protracted flushing attempt. They appear to be handling it well, although in a perfect world the pointer at the end of the line would be holding a higher tail. As an aside, pigeons are wonderful training birds; they're tough, they're inexpensive, they fly well, and most dogs will point them quite readily—although older dogs that have never been exposed to pigeons have been known to express their contempt for them in uniquely creative ways.

FEW SPORTSMEN—far too few—take the time to train during actual hunting situations. This is a mistake, for whether it's correcting breaches of etiquette or reinforcing desirable behaviors, there's a sense in which your dog should *always* be in training. Look at it as an investment: It may entail some sacrifice today, but somewhere down the line it'll pay dividends. Plus, one of the cardinal rules of dog training is that the best time to correct a problem is the moment it develops—nipping it in the bud, so to speak—and if you maintain a laissez-faire attitude while hunting, you're going to have an even bigger problem on your hands by the time you finally get around to addressing it.

BECOMING ACCUSTOMED TO HORSES and learning to respond to a mounted handler are
part and parcel of the education of plantation quail dogs, which are required to range
boldly and gobble sizable chunks of country. By the same token, working dogs from
horseback is perhaps the best and easiest way to get them to extend their range. A horse
is also a great help in developing a consistently forward pattern, as it allows you to get to
a wayward dog quickly and physically turn it in the right direction. Every pointing dog
person should see what the view from the saddle looks like, because it truly is a new—
and frequently eye-opening—perspective.

As a GENERAL RULE, the continental breeds, like this Brittany, tend to retrieve more or less naturally, while the pointer and the various setters tend not to (although a fairly high percentage of Gordon setters are natural retrievers). Whether you make an issue of retrieving divides along much the same lines, with the owners of continental breeds typically arguing that it's indispensable and those in the pointer–setter camp attaching somewhat less importance to it. A commonly expressed sentiment among the latter goes something like this: "All I ask is that the dog help me find the bird. I can pick it up for myself." The interesting thing is that force-breaking to retrieve—a process that sounds much harsher than it usually is—often seems to awaken a dog's dormant instincts in this respect, transforming dogs that showed little interest in retrieving into some of the most enthusiastic and indefatigable retrievers of all.

THE LITERATURE OF GROUSE and woodcock hunting abounds with references to dogs that cheerfully retrieved the former but either flat out refused to retrieve the latter or would pick up a woodcock only to instantaneously spit it out (usually accompanied by an audible expression of distaste). Given the relish the canine race displays for carrion, excreta, and other items that turn our human stomachs, this behavior has always seemed a little puzzling; it just doesn't seem possible that a woodcock, especially one in feather, can taste that bad to an animal that puts the things into its mouth that a dog does. Well, the fact of the matter is that dogs that'll retrieve everything *but* woodcock occur a lot more frequently in fiction than they do in fact—and for a dog that has completed a force-breaking program to refuse to retrieve a woodcock, or any other game bird, is all but unheard of.

WHETHER YOU CONSIDER IT an element of the training process or something entirely separate, preseason conditioning is critical—just as it is for any endurance athlete. It builds stamina and cardiovascular capacity, toughens pads, burns off excess weight, reduces the incidence of joint and muscle injuries; in short, it gets your dogs into the physical shape they need to be in to withstand the rigors of the field and perform at peak efficiency. How you do it—roading from a truck, as pictured here, is just one of many methods—is less important than *that* you do it.

TIME WAS WHEN the only gear you needed to train a bird dog was a plain leather collar, a rope with a snap on one end, a whistle, and a shotgun. You could probably still train a dog with those bare essentials if you had to, but it wouldn't be nearly as much fun. And think of the contribution you're making to the GNP by investing in all those beepers, e-collars, vests, etc. It's a little known fact that the whole economy would grind to a halt if it weren't for the equipment purchased by pointing dog people.

BLESSED WITH ACUTE HEARING, dogs are able to detect a whistle blast at far greater ranges than humans are. Whether they respond to said blast, however, is the proverbial $64,000 question.

WHILE NSTRA TRIALS MAY BE geared toward the bird hunting rank and file, the competition is nonetheless intense. You'd better have your dog in tip-top shape, mentally and physically, if you expect to contend. Thorough preparation, of course, is essential—and, judging by the contents of this vehicle, the NSTRA participant who owns it is prepared for just about anything.

OF THE MANY CATEGORIES OF pointing dog field trials, those sponsored by NSTRA—the National Shoot-to-Retrieve Field Trial Association—are the most similar to real-world upland bird hunting and, in turn, the most accessible to the average sportsman. Basically, here's what you do in the NSTRA format: Grab your shotgun, turn loose your dog, and go bird hunting. All else equal, the more birds your dog points and retrieves within the allotted half-hour, the higher your score and the better your chances of winning a placement. Another of the reasons NSTRA has become so popular is that the dogs are not required to be steady to wing and shot, as they are in traditional field trials. This has essentially opened the door to working gun dogs, the overwhelming majority of which are allowed to break at flush.

EVERY KIND OF COMPETITION spawns its specialists, and NSTRA is no exception. There are NSTRA devotees who don't hunt at all but who run their dogs in trials virtually every week-end they're able to. The typical NSTRA dog, though, sees double duty as a hunting dog and field trial dog—just what the founders of the organization had in mind back in the late-1960s, when they envisioned shoot-to-retrieve field trials as a way for shoe-leather bird hunters to extend their season and get more enjoyment from their dogs.

IN THE NSTRA FORMAT, each productive point
receives a score, up to a maximum of 100, from one of
the two judges who follow the action. Style, intensity,
location, how quickly and emphatically the dog established point, and how resolutely it maintains its posture
through the flushing process all factor into the judge's
decision. Experienced NSTRA trialers shoot for scores
in the high 80s or low 90s, recognizing that a 95 is
about the highest score ever awarded.

EACH RETRIEVE in a NSTRA trial also receives a score on a 100-point scale, the chief criteria here being speed and completeness of delivery. You're allowed one step toward your dog without penalty, but any more than that results in a deduction. Fussing, dillydallying, or dropping the bird before bringing it to hand will result in lost points as well. The upshot is that if your dog's retrieving habits are sloppy—or if your dog is what's generously termed a "part-time retriever"—you're going to find yourself at a competitive disadvantage. The top NSTRA dogs retrieve like they've been shot out of a cannon.

BREED PARITY IS THE NORM in the shoot-to-retrieve realm, where literally every recognized pointing breed has earned placements and most have won championships. While it's true that pointers and English setters are the dominant forces, Brittanies and German shorthairs have been hugely successful in NSTRA as well, and *any* dog that covers the ground with a good turn of speed, points solidly, and retrieves reliably has a fighting chance to end up in the winner's circle.

ONE OF THE THINGS that makes the NSTRA format unique is that the scores are posted at the conclusion of each brace, so you know immediately if you're still in contention—or if you're free to pack up, head for home, and lick your wounds. Of course, this removes some of the drama from the proceedings and makes the announcement of the winners a bit anticlimactic. But it does nothing to lessen the elation you feel when a ribbon is pressed into your hands.

THE SOCIAL ASPECTS of field trials should not be overlooked. After the dogs have been cared for, after the winners have been congratulated and the losers consoled, it's time to relax, tell a story or two, and enjoy the camaraderie of like-minded sportsmen—sportsmen brought together by passions held in common and in trust.

THE HORSEBACK FIELD TRIAL is the classic field trial, the most traditional, definitive, and glamorous form of bird dog competition. And while horseback trials are contested from New England to the Pacific Northwest and from Canada to Mexico—and while they're run on a variety of game birds, from prairie chicken to chukar partridge—the sport's heart and soul remains in the Deep South, where, among the tall pines, the tawny sedge fields, and the swirling legends of their immortal ancestors, the finest pointers and English setters in America are put to the test on native bobwhite quail.

A TERRIFIC AMOUNT of organization and cooperation is required during the running of a horseback field trial. Simply stated, everybody needs to know their place. The handlers ride at the front, keeping a watchful eye on their dogs' whereabouts as they roam far and wide, often calling to them in elongated, vaguely musical whoops—singing, this is called—to keep them oriented to the course. The handlers are followed closely behind by the judges, usually two but sometimes three, whose daunting task it is to study the performance of each dog critically and dispassionately and determine the winners—and in a big trial this can mean looking at eighty, ninety, or even a hundred dogs over the course of a week or longer. Behind the judges ride the field trial marshal and his assistants; their job is to make sure everybody stays on the course and, in particular, that the mounted gallery (which follows behind them) doesn't crowd the judges, handlers, and dogs.

DOG WAGONS, often pulled by a matched pair of mules, typically bring up the rear of the field trial entourage. When trials are conducted on continuous courses, as those run on native quail invariably are, the dogs in upcoming braces have to be available on short notice—sort of like having a batter in the on-deck circle. The dog wagon, with eight or ten individual boxes, serves this purpose. It also gives the dogs that have completed their heats a ride home.

YOU'D BE SMILING, TOO, if you had a job that entailed riding a horse and fooling with bird dogs in some of the prettiest country God ever made.

PERHAPS NO ATHLETES ON EARTH combine speed, agility, and stamina—along with terrific courage and tenacity—to the degree that top-notch horseback field trial dogs do. They continually push the envelope, redefining the boundary between what is possible and what, for the time being, isn't. This seething athleticism becomes even more remarkable when you consider that it coexists with such a demanding level of training—although many field trial devotees will tell you that the most exciting dogs of all are those in whom this coexistence is at best a shaky truce.

THE RAISED CAP is the time-honored signal for a dog on point—and one of the most galvanizing, thrillingly evocative gestures in the field trial universe.

Judging a field trial is in many respects an unenviable task. Apart from the grueling physical demands imposed by long days in the saddle, it often requires drawing the finest distinctions—distinctions that may be indiscernible to those who don't possess the same wealth of knowledge, the same depth and breadth of experience. Which is to say, the determination of the winners is rarely cut-and-dried, and for every handler who's rewarded, there are likely several who feel their dogs got the short end of the stick. Ultimately, a field trial judge must rely on the courage of his convictions and stand by his decisions regardless of how popular —or controversial—they may be.

The style and intensity of this pointer are beyond reproach, but the true test comes when the handler dismounts and begins his flushing attempt. Will the birds be accurately located—or will they have vanished? Will the dog maintain its poise and posture—or will it let down? Will it remain steady to wing and shot—or will it break? These are just some of the questions running through the minds not only of the handler and judges, but of everyone in the gallery. There are only a few scenarios in which everything goes right—and an infinite number of ways that it can all go hopelessly and irrevocably wrong.

THEIR CONSIDERABLE GLAMOUR and romance notwithstanding, field trials, for those who actively participate in them, are a lot like the famous definition of war: brief periods of chaos interrupted by long stretches of boredom. In a major stake with a big entry, it's not uncommon for a handler to go several days between appearances. Of course, a handler will do what work he can in these instances, roading his dogs from horseback to keep them in shape, even running them if he has access to grounds in the vicinity. Many handlers also like to ride as spectators—albeit spectators with a vested interest—noting where the coveys are being found, where they can show their dogs to best advantage, and whom they have to beat. Any way you slice it, though, field trials are largely a waiting game.

FOR A HANDLER who's confident he has a dog in contention, the minutes between the conclusion of the final brace and the announcement of the winners seem like hours. It's a struggle to keep your excitement in check, to temper your breathless hopes—hopes built not just on a single shining hour, but on years of hard, patient work—with the knowledge that disappointment is always a possibility. When the names that emerge from the judge's mouth are those of you and your dog, the echo of their sound buoyed atop the spontaneous applause, it feels, for a moment, like a dream. But then you know it's real, and that no matter what the costs, what the sacrifices, what the heartbreak—with dogs, there is always heartbreak—it was worth it.

MORE THAN HALF A CENTURY AGO, the revered outdoor writer Nash
Buckingham declared that the spirit of American field trials is "an incredible and intangible longing." The world has changed dramatically since
he made that observation—and, in the estimation of sportsmen fighting a
rear-guard battle to preserve an ever dwindling supply of game (along with
the very right to hunt), not for the better. The capacity of field trials and
the dogs they exalt to stir the imagination, however, remains undimmed,
secure in a place beyond the erosive reach of time.